JVC
MAKE YOUR
HOME VIDEO
MORE PROFESSIONAL

David Owen

foulsham

LONDON • NEW YORK • TORONTO • SYDNEY

foulsham

Yeovil Road, Slough, Berkshire SL1 4JH

ISBN 0–572–01151–2

Copyright © 1990 David Owen

Commissioning Editor: David Sarjent

Printed in Great Britain at Cambus Litho, East Kilbride

CONTENTS

THE EQUIPMENT

Video was originally developed for professional use, so that programmes could be recorded and edited when convenient, or could be repeated at reasonable intervals, freeing broadcasters from the tyranny of all-live production. Since then, it has developed into a deservedly popular and successful branch of the home entertainment industry. Not only can we watch programmes we would otherwise never see, we can watch feature films at home, thanks to being able to buy or to hire pe-recorded tapes as an alternative to going to the cinema to watch the same productions on the big screen.

But the third phase of the so-called video revolution is, in many ways, the most exciting of all. This is the opportunity to make television programmes of our own. The flexibility and the sophistication of today's home video cameras and recorders have put home movie-making within everyone's reach. The combination of moving pictures in colour, with automatically synchronised sound and instant replay, means that video has no rival when it comes to recording and preserving a slice of reality – to be played back whenever you, and your audience, want.

It's true to say there's no real difficulty in learning to operate today's video equipment. More and more functions are being made automatic or semi-automatic, leaving the user to concentrate on the purely creative business of shooting and recording what he wants. But there are still lessons which ARE worth learning. The do's and dont's of making an entertaining film which is worth watching, apply with just as much force to making video programmes. Lighting your subject, framing your shots properly, telling the story through the accepted grammar of movie-making – all are essential in the making of a home video which looks and sounds thoroughly professional.

Today's equipment is capable of delivering better and better pictures in terms of sharpness and realism – so it's now worthwhile, more than ever, to learn how to be a professional director, producer, cameraman, sound recordist, and editor. That is the purpose of this book – read on, and you may well be surprised by how much you enjoy learning the craft of movie-making.

Today's video cameras and recorders really do offer amazing value for money. For a few hundred pounds apiece, you can buy equipment which does just the same job as a professional, broadcast-quality camera or recorder costing ten or even a hundred times as much. There are differences, of course. The kit used by television companies is more complex because it either uses a wider tape format, or the tape runs at a higher speed so that there's a larger area of tape, on which the picture information is stored. There are all kinds of circuits and features designed to enhance picture quality and improve sharpness, to cope with low light levels and high-contrast subjects, and a hundred and one other things.

But at the end of the day, the home-video enthusiast with his VHS-C camera will be looking for the same qualities in his shots as the professional TV cameraman – or he should be. The fact that the picture quality will be slightly less sharp with the cheaper camera matters less than the fact that the pictures you shoot really will be your own: unique, a part of your own life and your own inspiration in a way that even the best broadcast television programme can never be. In short, making your own video is a genuinely active and creative pastime, in contrast to the purely passive role of watching other people's programmes on your television set.

However, there is one point you need to bear in mind when travelling from one country to another. Different nations use different television systems – the USA and Canada use the NTSC system, the UK and West Germany use the PAL system, France uses the SECAM system and so on. This means you can buy a camcorder in America, and play back the recorded tape through an American TV set, but you can't play it back through a normal TV set in the UK, France or West Germany, for example. As a general principle, it is best to buy a camcorder on your own home market. Then you can use it anywhere in the world, operating from its rechargeable batteries, and still play back the tapes on your own TV set when you return home.

So let's begin by looking at the two halves of your production equipment: the camera and the recorder.
With the introduction of the Video Eight format, which uses a narrow eight-millimetre wide magnetic tape, and compact VHS which uses a smaller version of the VHS cassettes used on most domestic video recorders, cameras and recorders are usually sold as a single unit. The advantages are in size and weight. It's now perfectly practical for shooting and recording to be a genuinely one-man operation. The disadvantages are that Video Eight has to be copied on to VHS for playback on a normal recorder, while the miniature VHS used in portable camcorders can be played back directly by fitting them into a special adapter to fit the larger domestic machines.

The latest cameras offer even more features and possibilities, to match the newest models of video recorders now on the market. For example, there are cameras which can record on a VHS cassette

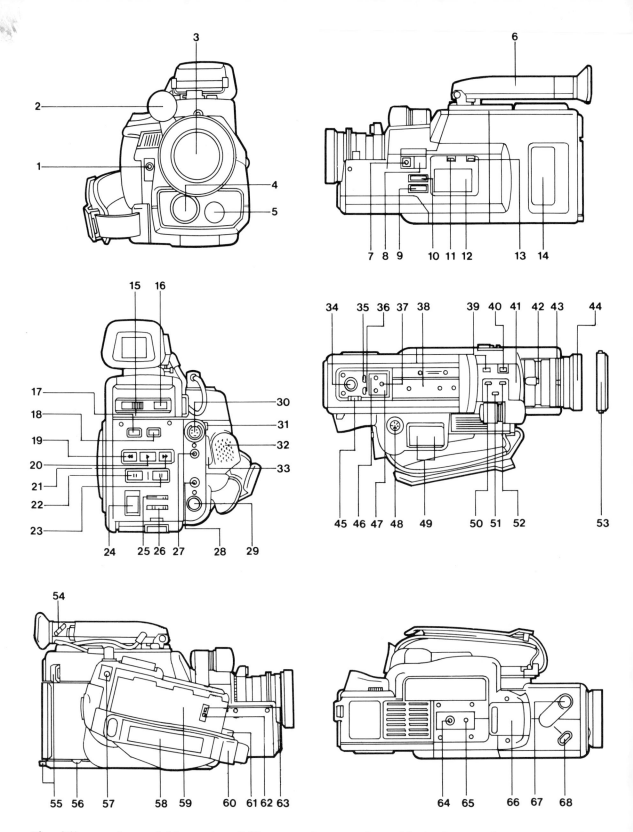

The different views of this modern JVC camcorder, together with the key on the page opposite, reveal the level of sophistication now available to the enthusiast.

1	External microphone jack (MIC)	35	Date/time on/off button
2	Exclusive microphone	36	Recording time reset button
3	Zoom lens	37	Date/time mode button
4	Auto-focus sensor window	38	Viewfinder mount
5	White balance sensor window	39	Page button
6	Electronic viewfinder	40	Title on/off button
7	Full auto button	41	Manual zoom lever
8	Focus select button	42	Macro button
9	Shutter select button	43	Manual focus ring
10	White balance select button	44	Lens hood
11	Counter memory button	45	Recording time on/off switch
12	Liquid crystal display (LCD)	46	Date/time select button
13	Counter reset button	47	Date/time set button
14	Cassette holder	48	Viewfinder cable connector
15	Power switch	49	Power zoom buttons
16	Recording standby button	50	Image reverse button
17	Monitor button	51	Title memory button
18	Quick review/edit button	52	Colour button
19	Rewind/shuttle search button	53	Lens cap
20	Play button	54	Dioptric adjustment control
21	Fast forward/shuttle search button	55	Slots for shoulder strap
22	Pause/still button	56	Tracking control
23	Stop button	57	DC In terminal
24	Eject switch	58	Grip strap
25	Standard play/long play recording mode select switch	59	Battery mount
26	Dubbing on/off switch	60	Lens cap hook
27	Remote control jack	61	Battery pack release lever
28	Earphone jack	62	Video Out Switch
29	AV connector	63	S-VHS switch
30	S-video out connector	64	Tripod mounting socket
31	Alarm on/off switch	65	Stud hole
32	Thumb rest	66	Clock battery compartment
33	Recording start/stop button	67	Back light compensation button
34	Second recording start/stop button	68	Fader button

using either the normal VHS format, or the newer S–VHS format, which relies on a higher-frequency carrier wave to produce a sharper picture, with improved horizontal resolution. Some cameras have a tape speed switch which allows you to record or play back at standard speed (SP) or the slower long-play speed (LP) – for a slight drop in picture quality, you can record six hours of material on a normal three-hour tape. And the latest models have a feature of even greater importance to the home-video producer – they can act as the input half of an edit system when wired up to your home video recorder, allowing you to edit a finished programme from the sequences you record with the camera, in the same way as professionals build up complete programmes shot by shot.

In all these cases, though, the camera and the ordinary mains video recorder do the same job. The camera's role is essentially the same as that of a movie camera – or for that matter the more familiar kind of camera for taking still snapshots. It uses its lens to focus an image of the object at which it's pointed. But instead of focusing this image on to a film where it can be recorded chemically, it focusses it on to a screen where the different parts of the picture are transformed into electrical signals.

These electrical signals are passed to the recorder, which then records them onto the magnetic tape in the video cassette, in exactly the same way as sound signals can be recorded on to magnetic tape in an audio tape-recorder or cassette recorder. Once the recording is finished, the videotape cassette can be played back on any recorder. The signals obtained from the original picture will then re-create that picture on the television screen – rather as the signals from a broadcast television transmitter are received by a television aerial and fed down a cable to the set to be reassembled into a picture.

This gives video its two most obvious advantages over film as a medium for recording moving pictures. First, because the picture information is recorded on to the videotape magnetically, it's available for instant replay at any time. That means you can see what a shot looks like while there's still time to reshoot it if need be; waiting for ciné film to be developed and processed could take days or even weeks. Second, the magnetic tape is completely reusable. This means if the shot isn't quite as you wanted it, you can not only reshoot it straight away, but you can record it over the same part of the tape, so that you only take home the material you're completely happy with.

Until recently today's cameras were based on the shoulder-mounted cameras used by professional television cameramen when out on location, where portability is important. Known in the trade as the 'Iron Parrot', the shoulder-mounted camera has two advantages. It's less tiring to use, even with the larger and heavier professional cameras, and it's easier to obtain steady shots when a tripod isn't available, or when there's no time to set one up. Because they are still smaller and lighter than their predecessors, the latest camera/recorders have reverted back to the hand-held models, similar to the small home-movie cine-cameras which were popular before the video revolution. Like them, they need careful handling, *because* they are so light – check the instructions in the owner's manual about the right way to hold them and reach all the controls, most of which can be operated by one hand. But always use your other hand to help steady the camera, whilst making any other adjustments, like changing the focus, otherwise it is all too easy for camera-shake to mar your carefully-planned shots without you realising it until afterwards. We'll look at this in more detail later.

You'll notice straight away some very obvious differences from a typical home-movie cine-camera. The lens system will look much the same, but instead of an optical viewfinder, your video camera will have an electronic viewfinder: basically a very small black-and-white TV set which shows you exactly the picture the lens will be recording, with only the colour missing. There will also be a set of buttons on a control panel which look after various camera functions. For example, one of them will control the focusing arrangements, to adjust the lens to produce a sharp picture, depending on the distance between you and the subject. Many of today's video cameras have an automatic focus facility. All you have to do is sight the camera so that the subject you want to shoot is seen against a ring marking at the centre of the screen, and the camera will focus automatically.

There are times when this can be useful – as when following an object which is approaching you or receding from you, without the need to readjust the focus manually to take this into account. But in most cases, you'll need the extra control you have by setting the focus manually. Turning the focus adjustment ring on the lens barrel gives you a greater degree of control when you're shooting. In that case, you'll need to select 'manual' on the focus-mode controls on the side of the camera.

Setting up to record a shot is simplicity itself with today's cameras. All you need do, after loading a cassette into the recorder part of the machine, and selecting the camera controls rather than the recorder controls, is to hold the camera as shown in the handbook, slipping your right hand through the loop on the outside of the lens mounting. This places your right hand next to the stop/start button, and the rocker switch which controls the zoom lens. You press the button to start the camera recording, and press it again to stop – it's as simple as that. But there are one or two other adjustments and controls you will need to come to terms with first.

It's important to understand that video recorders shouldn't be left in the 'pause' mode for too long. There are two reasons for this. The tape, and the recording heads may become damaged, and the batteries will run out that much faster. So most cameras have a safety device which automatically goes into the 'stop' mode if you leave the camera in 'pause' for more than a few minutes. The tape will be unlaced from the recording heads, and the picture will disappear from the viewfinder. If you find this has happened, when you want to record another shot, all you have to do is press the 'standby' button, and the picture will reappear in the viewfinder. Then you can select and frame your shot, and press the 'start' button to begin recording the next shot. Should you want to check what you've just been shooting there's usually a 'review' button which you can press, and the recorder will replay (through the viewfinder) the last two or three seconds of the previous shot.

If you want to play back any more of the recorded picture, you can use the normal 'rewind' and 'play' buttons on the recorder panel of your camera. But you will then need to switch back to the camera controls before shooting again. Normally, in a video camera the iris – the aperture of the lens which controls the amount of light entering the camera – operates automatically, which does at least save you the trouble of readjusting the lens aperture ring as the light level changes. But there is usually an override button which lets you shoot objects against a fairly bright background, which would other-wise appear as silhouettes. So long as you press the 'backlight' button, this facility operates. When you release it, the camera reverts to automatic-iris operating.

There's one other iris adjustment which is becoming increasingly common, and that's the 'fade' button. When this is pressed, it closes the iris down so that less and less light comes in through the lens, until all the light is cut off. The effect of this on the picture is to cause it to go darker and darker, until it eventually fades out completely to a black screen. Since a clever circuit fades the sound level down in keeping with the picture, this makes it a convenient device for ending a sequence, or a programme, or for implying the passing of time. Pressing the button again, when the lens aperture has been closed, allows the opposite process to take place. The picture fades up from a black screen, with the sound level rising as well. You can use this effect deliberately, to begin a programme, or you'll see later how a fade-out/fade-up in quick succession can be used as an effect which allows you to bridge a jump in location, or suggest the passing of time.

Finally, on most of today's cameras you'll find another invaluable lens adjustment: the zoom. This allows you to readjust the lens so that you can change the field of view of the camera. In other words, if you focus on a particular subject such as a boat on a lake, you have the choice of a wide shot which shows the boat as a small object in the distance with the lake and the surrounding countryside in the frame too. Or you can zoom right in to show the boat in close-up almost filling the frame, with just the water around it and none of the wider surroundings in the shot. Between these two extremes, you can frame the picture anywhere you like by adjusting the zoom, and you can actually zoom in and out as part of the shot itself. Some cameras have manual zoom adjustments, where you can zoom in and out by turning another ring on the lens barrel – but most now tend to have a power zoom, driven by an electric motor and controlled by a rocker switch to move in and out at will, with the pressure on the switch determining the speed of the zoom. Next come the controls which determine the way in which the picture seen through the lens is turned into the electrical signals sent to the video recorder part of the combination.

The most important control is the white balance. This adjusts the camera's response to the colours of the objects being shot, depending on the kind of light in which they're seen. For example, clear daylight does in fact have a slightly blue cast, while tungsten lighting indoors has a distinctly yellowish quality. To the naked eye, objects seen in these two different conditions may appear exactly the same, because the human eye compensates for them quite automatically. But unless the balance between the camera's response to the different colours is adjusted to take this difference into account, the colours of the played-back picture will appear distinctly odd.

For example, a camera set up for daylight shooting would show an indoor scene shot under tungsten lighting as much yellower than the scene would appear to the naked eye. In the same way, a camera set up for the same conditions and used in daylight would record a picture with a definite blue cast, compared with what the human eye would see without the camera.

This means the camera has to be set up to compensate for the kind of light in which the pictures are being shot – and this is the purpose of the white balance controls. In the latest cameras, this adjustment is simple. All you have to do is press a 'white balance' button several times until the viewfinder display shows you the symbol which matches the conditions under which you are shooting – daylight, fluorescent light, or normal domestic-type tungsten-filament lighting. On some models you can even choose an automatic white-balance option which not only sets the camera for the conditions in which you are recording at the time, but will compensate for different conditions if you go in and out of doors, or if the light begins to fade towards evening, for example.

Using the zoom lens: three shots taken with the camera in the same position. This is with the lens zoomed out to show a wide shot . . .

This is midway through the range of the zoom . . .

And this is zoomed in to show the narrowest picture area, filling the whole frame.

Finally, the camera will have a facility which allows you to record a new shot at whatever point on the preceding shot you want to add it – in what is called an 'assemble edit'. Assuming that the camera and recorder have been turned off since the previous shot, this means that you have to switch the system on, wait five seconds for the tape to thread itself around the heads and for a picture to appear in the viewfinder. Then you wait till you reach the point at which you want the new shot to begin, and press the 'pause' button. From that point, everything is set up for the new shot.

When you're ready to record, all you need do is press the 'record' button, followed by the 'start' button and the new shot will begin recording at the right point on the tape, with a smooth edit which allows you to build up a complete programme shot by shot. It also allows you to go back to record a shot over an unsatisfactory attempt at the same shot. So, by carefully reviewing what you've recorded (subject to the battery life you have left, which will be displayed inside the viewfinder) you can make sure that the programme material you build up is as good as time and trouble will allow. When you've finished, save batteries by going into 'standby' and then switch off.

The correct way to hold a camera. Remember it is very easy to let the camera move up or down and so ruin the picture; whenever possible, a camera support should be used or improvised from a wall, a fence, a branch or whatever is available.

Now let's assume that you're going to try shooting some pictures. First of all, you need to make sure that everything is connected up correctly, according to the operating manual for the equipment you're using. This means checking the batteries or the connections to the mains supply or even your car battery, depending on the power source you're using, and that the power-zoom adjustment and the electronic viewfinder are connected to the camera proper.

Switch the machine on, make sure you have a tape in the recorder (surprisingly easy to forget, when you're concentrating on the camera adjustments!) Check that it's wound back to the beginning, and that the pip which allows recording is in place. Turn to the camera controls and set the camera into the 'recording stand-by' mode. Set the automatic white balance controls according to whether you're shooting outdoors in daylight, or indoors under artificial light. Make sure the focus adjustment has been set to 'manual'. Now you're almost ready to shoot.

The first thing to check is that you're holding the camera correctly. This will depend on the type of camera you have, but the essential thing is to make sure you're holding it as still and as steady as possible without being too tense, and to make sure you can reach all the controls. For the shoulder-mounted cameras, this means resting the camera where it feels comfortable, and then adjusting the position of the viewfinder, so that you can see the picture clearly without craning or twisting your neck. On this type of camera, there's usually a handle for your right hand with a safety strap which fits round your wrist. For the newer, smaller hand-held cameras, you still fit your right hand into the safety strap which allows you to operate the zoom controls with your fingers and the start/stop button with your thumb. But you hold the camera in front of you rather than alongside you, which means you have to remember to make a positive effort to hold it steady while shooting.

If the camera is fitted with a power zoom, the rocker switch can be operated by your first and second fingers. Pressing with your index finger pushes down the rearmost half of the rocker switch and causes the lens to zoom out, or appear to pull back away from the subject. Pressing with your second finger on the front half of the switch causes the lens to zoom in, towards the subject. Usually you can operate the start-stop button with your right thumb, pressing once to stop the recording, and pressing again to restart it. This leaves your left hand free to help steady the camera, to change the focus when this is needed (remembering to keep your left hand well clear of the lens), or to press the 'backlight' or 'fade' buttons.

Now choose a subject – preferably, at this stage, a subject which isn't going to cause problems by suddenly starting to move, and preferably something which is neither too near nor too far away. Let's say, for example, that we begin by looking at a parked car. Point the camera at the subject, and look at it through the viewfinder. The chances are that the image will be fuzzy and out of focus. Use your left hand to move the focussing ring of the lens until the car appears clear and sharp.

Now, holding the camera as steadily as you can, press the stop/start button. The camera will now be recording, and you can usually check this in the viewfinder by seeing a 'record' light or LCD symbol illuminate, or begin flashing steadily. On the more sophisticated cameras, there will be other warning lights inside the viewfinder, where you can't miss them, however hard you may be concentrating on your shooting – one to warn you that the batteries are getting low, another to tell you the light level is too low for good results, and sometimes another to tell you that you're nearing the end of the tape. We won't concern ourselves with these other lights just now – but you need to watch out for any of these warnings as your shooting proceeds.

Now try pressing the front of the rocker switch, and zoom in to a close-up of the car – if your camera has a manual zoom adjustment, this means turning the zoom ring with your left hand so as to close in to a close-up of the car. Depending on the distance between you and the car, and the power of your lens, this may mean that you're looking at the whole car, or just the bonnet and windscreen, or even at the window of the driver's door. Whichever it is, you should be aware of two things – the chances are that the picture which you carefully focused to begin with has now drifted out of focus again, so that the image is fuzzy. Use your left hand to readjust the focus ring to make the picture crisp and sharp again, and then you'll notice the second difference. Now that you're in close-up, the effect of any slight movement of the camera will be much more obvious.

Now press on the rearmost edge of the rocker switch (or turn the zoom ring in the opposite direction) and the lens will zoom out. You'll see the car recede and grow smaller in the viewfinder as if you're moving away from it. *You're* not, of course. The effect is a purely optical one, created in the movement of the different components of the lens.

When the lens has zoomed out as far as it will go, look closely at the picture again. You should notice two more things about this shot, apart from the fact that the car (or the part of the car) which filled the frame of the viewfinder before, now occupies only a very small part of the picture. You're seeing the rest of the car, both sides of the road, some of the pavement and the surrounding buildings as well. But the picture has remained in focus. Because you refocused it when you were zoomed into the subject close-up, the picture has in fact stayed sharp all the way out to the long shot. (That's the name for the opposite of a close-up, though to be slightly confusing, it's sometimes called a wide shot as well; we'll explain that a little later.) And the second thing? Provided you're holding the camera as carefully and as steadily as you were before, you should see that the effects of any movements of the camera are much less obvious than they were in close-up.

When your picture's out of focus, turn the focus ring on the lens . . .

Until the subject comes into sharp focus.

Many cameras also have a 'Macro' facility on the lens which allows you to focus on a subject which is much closer than the normal limit of the lens – right up to the lens surface itself in some instances. In this case, you press a special 'Macro' button, and then use the manual-zoom control to bring your subject into sharp focus. You can even pull back all the way in a normal zoom by moving the manual adjustment right back to the opposite extreme of the range, giving you a longer than normal zoom-out option from an extremely close-range subject.

Of course, the zoom lens is only one way to move from one kind of picture to another. Another way is to carry out a 'pan'. Let's say in this example that we're going to pan from our original parked car to one which is parked a little further along the road. Press the remote control button to cause the recorder to pause. Now try looking through the viewfinder as you frame up the first car properly. This means using the rocker switch (or the zoom ring) to zoom back in until the car almost fills the frame.

Panning from one subject to another, to link them in the same shot. Here the camera pans from the signal box . . .

Across the railway tracks . . .

To the signal.

Now try holding the camera very steadily, and swing slowly around till you can see the second car in the viewfinder. Check the framing – is this subject properly framed and still in sharp focus? If it isn't, pick another subject which avoids these difficulties. If it is, then go back to the first car, and try slowly pivoting round, looking through the viewfinder until the second car comes into view – then stop. This is a pan. If you were swinging round to the left from the first car to the second, then it's a pan to the left, or PAN LEFT in a script. The other way, and it's a PAN RIGHT.

But you're not limited to level movements to left and right. Let's imagine that you wanted to make a point by shifting from the car to show one of the overhead lamp standards. This would mean a different, and perhaps more difficult, camera movement where you move upwards from the car until the overhead lamp comes into view. But the principles are still the same. Try the shot out first in slow motion, so that you do end up with your chosen subject in the frame. It's all too easy to get the camera movement nice and smooth, and miss your target altogether – one safeguard is to keep your other eye open so that you can compare the real scene with the picture in the viewfinder, to check any drift off-target. You'll also need to check that the focus is still sharp. Now you can return to the car, line up the shot, brace yourself to hold the camera as steadily as possible, and press the start button. Give the shot a second or so to establish itself and then tilt the camera upwards until you find the overhead light. Then stop, wait a second or so, and press the stop/start button again to stop the recording.

This kind of shot is sometimes called a PAN UP, sometimes a TILT UP. Now you can try starting the shot on the overhead light and panning (or tilting) down to the car. That's a PAN (or TILT) DOWN. The main point of trying all these different shots at this stage is to get you accustomed to operating the camera, to holding it smoothly, and to making the kind of movements which will bring pace and variety to your shooting.

But now we reach the acid test. It's time to take a look at what you've recorded. Depending on the type of camera you have, it may or may not be possible to play back the tape and watch the picture in the camera viewfinder. But the best way is to take it back to base and play it back through the television set. This will mean you'll see your pictures in colour, and you'll see them on a large enough screen to show up all the blemishes and imperfections, and you'll save your batteries.

Be prepared for a shock. We all of us tend to spend a good deal of time watching television made by professionals, on very costly equipment, and sparing no effort or expense to produce a smooth and glossy result, from the technical point of view at least. Your picture quality WILL fall short of that kind of standard, but the fact that it shows *your* neighbourhood and what *you've* just been shooting gives it a special kind of immediacy, and a special kind of excitement. Try looking at it objectively, and don't be discouraged at this stage. Look for faults so that you can learn how to correct them later, as your skill and experience improve and you become more professional.

First of all, you'll probably be surprised at how shaky the picture seems. The slightest camera movement seems distracting, because it's unexpected, and because it seems a great deal more unsteady than it does in real life. When we look at a subject with the naked eye, we're not aware of our own head or body movements, because we tend to compensate for them automatically, and because we don't concentrate quite as hard on our field of view. But the television screen tends to focus our attention very closely indeed. We tend to notice every detail of the subject, and this close concentration cannot help spotting every shift of the camera and every movement of the lens.

Watch specially for the pans from subject to subject. Unless you have some experience, or have a natural aptitude for this kind of shot – which is MOST unusual – you'll probably find they don't work too well at first. If you pan too quickly, all you'll tend to have is a confused blur once you move off the first subject, until you reach the second. To be successful, a pan has to be much slower than you could transfer your gaze from the first object to the second using your own eyes. Second, even if the pace is right, you'll probably find the start and stop of the pan are jerky and distracting. What you must strive for is a smooth transition from the beginning of the shot (where the camera is stationary) into the pan itself, and an equally smooth transition from the end of the pan to the end of the shot, where the camera is still once again, this time concentrating on the second subject.

What's needed is actually a very slow acceleration, so that you start off the pan very slowly and build up gradually to the movement to the second subject. In the same way, as you reach the end of the shot, you have to slow down progressively, so that you can stop with the subject perfectly in the frame, without jerking the camera and without overshooting and having to pan back. Those are the hallmarks of the amateur, and they're surprisingly difficult to eliminate. The only answer is practice, so that moving slowly, steadily, and smoothly from shot to shot becomes second nature: a completely automatic response which allows you to concentrate on the subjects which form the beginning and end of the shot.

This is probably even more true of shots which involve tilting up and down, since this involves a more difficult movement. Here again the secret is to try to move yourself and the camera as a combination, rather than simply tilting the camera up and down. Lean backwards from the waist as you tilt up, and bend forwards from the waist as you tilt down – and keep the camera as steady as possible when you do it. Finally, remember that the same speeding up and slowing down process should be applied at the start and end of a zoom shot in either direction.

Now go and try the same practice session out again, bearing these points in mind. Record the results, and see how much better they look when you play them back. Keep trying till you can see a genuine improvement. Then you'll be ready to try . . .

People in long shot (LS). A medium shot might show two or three of the crowd in the frame, a close-up a single person, a big close-up might show a face, and an extreme close-up the eyes or mouth. But all these terms are relative.

CALLING THE SHOTS

chapter 2

In the previous chapter you learned how to operate the camera, how to use features like the zoom lens, and how to make simple camera movements like panning and tilting, to move from one subject to another. The next step is to consider the different types of shot, so that you can understand what is meant by a long shot, a wide shot, or an extreme close-up.

Once you understand these definitions, and can recognise them, then it's possible to work out how to tell a story, or to put over a message, in a logical and interesting sequence of shots. And when you can decide what kind of shot a particular subject calls for at a particular moment, then you can decide exactly how it should be framed, to suit the sequence and to make the shot itself as clear, and as attractive as possible. So first find yourself a subject which you can shoot from some distance away – for example, a group of three people sitting on a seat on the other side of the road. Set up your camera, zoom in as close as possible to the group, and then adjust the focus for a sharp picture.

Depending on the distance between you and the group, and the power of the lens of your camera, you may see all three people in the viewfinder – or you may see just one. Either way, this is best described as a CLOSE-UP. If you then operate the zoom so that the lens zooms back from the group as far as possible, so that they occupy only part of the picture, along with the surrounding scene, this now becomes a LONG SHOT. If you now zoom back in to around halfway between the two, then you have a MEDIUM SHOT. Broadly speaking, those are the three basic types of shot for a given subject.

But that's just the beginning. If you were shooting this subject for a genuine programme, or with a camera having a more powerful zoom lens, then your range of possible shots would be much greater. If you wanted a bigger close-up than your lens would allow, then you might even consider moving your camera closer to the subject to get the shot you wanted. So these three descriptions aren't nearly detailed enough. Let's look a little closer. Literally. Let's say, once again, that our subject is three people sitting and talking on a roadside seat. Imagine that the programme you are shooting demands that we see the face of one particular person, to concentrate our attention to him or her rather than the others. Usually, this would be classified as a CLOSE-UP. But imagine that you now want to move in closer, to emphasise the facial expression even more closely. You zoom in closer by moving the camera or by using the zoom, until the frame merely shows their eyes, nose and mouth, clipping off their neck and the top of their head. This is now a BIG CLOSE-UP. If you want to move in closer still, to concentrate on the eyes, then you're going for an EXTREME CLOSE-UP. As explained below, all these terms are relative.

The same graduation between one type of shot and another happens as you zoom out, or move the camera back away from the subject. Move back out far enough from the group to see all three figures, and you have what might be described as a MEDIUM CLOSE-UP – halfway between our CLOSE-UP and our MEDIUM SHOT. Move back further still, and you have the MEDIUM SHOT we looked at earlier. Further back again, and we're looking at a MEDIUM LONG-SHOT and finally, with the subject at the maximum distance away, we're back at a LONG SHOT. Or, in certain circumstances, it's called a WIDE SHOT; there's no hard and fast rule about which term you use.

Generally speaking, it depends on the context. If what strikes you most forcibly as you pull back from the subject is the increasing distance separating you from the subject, then a LONG SHOT is the description that suits the image you see. But sometimes the surroundings may have a different effect. You may be more conscious of the scenery or the surroundings in which the subject is placed, so that it's more logical to describe it as a WIDE SHOT.

In fact, you'll see that these terms are anything but rigid. They have to be capable of being used to suit any kind of subject and any kind of variation between EXTREME CLOSE-UP and EXTREME LONG-SHOT of that subject. In some cases, you may use a different set of definitions to make the distinction clear.

Before we look at the problems of choosing and framing individual shots to make the best of a subject, there's one other kind of shot description which is worth knowing about. It's used in interviews, in drama, or in any other situation where people are talking to one another.

It works like this. Let's imagine now that our three people are in conversation. One of them is an interviewer, and the other two are answering his questions. You may want to introduce the group by a shot which shows the trio filling the frame. This is often described as a THREE-SHOT. You may want to concentrate on the interviewer, in which case you follow it with a CLOSE-UP (INTERVIEWER). Then you may want to show the reactions of both the interviewees to one of his questions but, for variety, you don't want to see the whole group again. So this time you frame the shot so that you can only see the two people being interviewed, in which case – logically enough – it's a TWO-SHOT. If you go back to the group, it's a THREE-SHOT again, and then if you concentrate on one person answering a single question then it's another CLOSE-UP, and so on.

It's important to remember that these shot descriptions are just that: shorthand classifications to indicate a type of shot rather than a hard and fast definition of how a shot should be set up and framed. Because in the end how you compose a shot depends on you: the camera operator. It can be a matter of inspiration; on the other hand, there are guidelines which can be learned to help you get it right. Keep to these, and in time framing will become second nature to you. But always, above all, keep a weather eye open for the unusual, the interesting, or the unexpected. Remember that an unusual view of a familiar sight is worth taking a little extra trouble over.

So let's start setting up some shots. To begin with, look for static subjects – coping with moving ones is a special technique we'll come to later.

This time we're not looking for a single subject which we'll treat in different ways between a long shot and a close-up, as we did before. Instead, we should be looking for different types of subject, so that we can explore the different types of framing which will draw attention to different facets of each subject.

Take a typical family outing, when video enthusiasts seem to be everywhere – a visit to a steam railway, or a main-line steam excursion. Trains make splendid subjects, but like any other public function in the open air, so do people. People enjoying themselves, people relaxing, people paying rapt attention to whatever it is they've come to see, people talking, people dozing, people reading, people working, or people sheltering from the rain. They're all of them potential material for your camera in different ways.

Let's begin with a train, waiting to depart. If you want a shot of the engine, then find yourself a suitable vantage point, and think how you're going to compose the shot. If you stand sideways on to the engine, you find yourself encountering the first problem of video shooting. You can't crop the finished picture to suit the subject, as you can with a photograph: you always have to work within the confines of the television screen, and its proportion of height to breadth. So a subject like a side view of a train or a steam engine is going to have a lot of space above and below the subject left vacant. This is fine if what you want is a shot of the train in its context – against a background of a green hillside, or the complex tracery of a station roof. But if your interest is the engine itself, pure and simple, then try and find a different viewpoint which will fill your frame more easily. Move round to one end of the engine, so that its length appears foreshortened, and the height and width of your subject looks better suited to the proportions of the screen – and therefore those of the viewfinder through which you're studying it.

Subject in medium shot (MS).

Subject in close-up (CU).

Subject in big close-up (BCU).

Subject in extreme close-up (ECU).

Let's assume that you're now standing somewhere in front of the engine and over to one side. If what you want to show in your shot is the whole engine, then all you need do is frame your shot so that there is enough of a border around the engine to fix it in context.

Try to think of the pictures and prints and photographs of steam engines you may have seen in magazines or in shop windows, and compose your shot in a similar way. Artists usually try to avoid placing the focus of the picture right in the middle – where the horizontal and vertical centre-lines of the picture converge – and this too is worth bearing in mind. But pulling back a little to show something of the background is usually worthwhile.

Try zooming back and compare the effect of including some of the watching crowd, part of the tracks down which the engine and train will be moving, something of the bustle on the platform. It's not as necessary with video to capture the whole essence of the scene in a single shot, as it would be for the artist or the photographer, since one picture of the scene they're recording is all you're ever likely to see. In any film or television programme, the scene will be followed by all kinds of other shots, showing different details and different perspectives, and once you're happy that the main shot – what's often called the establishing shot – has done its job adequately, then it's time to look for some of these follow-up shots.

Here you need an eye for the unexpected. What kind of expressions, activities, details look interesting or intriguing? Why is the fireman of the engine walking round to the front to change the position of the lamps? Zoom in more closely so that you're framed around the front end of the engine so that he, and what he's doing, fills the picture. What about the small boys staring into the cab to watch the driver? A close-up of the faces so that everything in the frame spells fascination, concentration, absorption?

25

You can explain what it is they're looking at in the next shot, by turning round and using the camera to show their view of the subject – a shot of the cab, with the driver drinking a cup of tea, perhaps. If what they're waiting for is the signal for departure, then a shot of the signal arm still showing 'danger' is another possibility. Already you and your camera are setting a scene and telling a story, entirely in pictures and the order in which you're finding the different subjects and the way in which you're shooting them.

This time, we said we'd confine ourselves to essentially static subjects – so we'll carry on recording the scene to the moment where the train pulls out. So keep looking for other subjects which will help remind you of the place and what was happening, when you view what you've recorded, back at home.

What about the piles of luggage on the platform, passengers climbing into the coaches, doors being slammed, the colourful advertisements on the station platform? Is there anything else which tells you that departure is imminent? What about the driver looking out for the signal, or steam being released?

In this case it's essential to come in close on the source of the noise to explain to your audience what's causing it. Look out for the signal changing to 'clear', or the guard standing on the platform with his flag and whistle, perhaps looking at his watch. All these shots help build up towards the drama of departure, but you could well end the sequence looking at the engine from behind, so that part of the picture shows the tracks down which the train will be going once departure time comes.

That is just one example of how a location can be used to tell a story in a series of imaginative shots, to cover both the essential ingredients of what's happening, interspersed with some of the more unexpected details. It's a difficult assignment, because unless the camera operator is unusually lucky, there will only be a limited time to capture the shots which are needed, before the train leaves and changes the scene beyond all recognition. So let's turn our attention now to a different kind of scene, where the major ingredients which go to make it up aren't likely to change or disappear for a long time. One useful example might be a visit to a stately home – not simply for the house and garden itself, since these are essentially static subjects, but as the scene for a particular function – like a vintage car rally.

This immediately suggests two parts of the subject which need to be shot: the cars themselves, the people who have brought them and come to see them, and the house and estate as a setting for the event. A well-chosen wide shot can include both, and can effectively set the scene for all the details and close-ups and facets which you will find to record later. But take some time to find a viewpoint which will allow a slightly more imaginative treatment than a statically framed shot. If this is going to be a really long shot, which it may well have to be to capture a large showground full of vehicles and a big house in the distance, then any movement in the picture is likely to be small and insignificant in terms of what you're showing in the frame. So why not put one of the movements we looked at in the previous chapter to good use, to link the two parts of the scene in a single shot?

You might try to pan from the house (which is a normal and predictable part of a landscape like this) across to a field full of beautifully kept motor cars – which is unexpected in this context. This would depend on the relative positions of the two parts of your shot. They would need to be far enough apart for the cars not to be obvious at the start of your shot, and for the house to be out of sight at the end of it. But you don't want too long a pan to link the two parts of your shot, as this is difficult to maintain and the shot might tend to become boring.

Now suppose that the limitations of the site are such that you can't see the cars without the house in the background. Then you might try to zoom out from some small but recognisable detail of the house which tells you what kind of house it is – let's say a Georgian doorway, and a drive sweeping up to it. Pick a camera position which will allow you to zoom in and pick up this kind of subject in close-up at the end of your zoom. Then zoom out slowly to the widest end of the zoom, and see what kind of picture you have. If you can then see the field full of cars in the foreground, with the house now a much smaller part of the picture in the distant background, then you will have achieved the same link in a different way. But you might well have to try several different camera positions before the picture at both ends of your zoom are as you want them.

Of course, it's equally possible to use the zoom in as a linking shot in the same way. If your intention is to take the field full of cars as your starting point, but you want to emphasise that the gathering is in fact a competition event, then you need to find some small detail in the scene which will make this point as clearly and as neatly as possible.

Perhaps there is a rosette on the windscreen of one of the cars which has been assessed as a winner in one of the classes, but is standing in the field among many others which haven't won a prize. Now you need to work the shot in reverse. Find a camera position which allows you to show the windscreen and the rosette large enough in frame at the close-up end of the zoom, for everyone to be

A side-view shot of a train doesn't fill the frame well, since the linear shape of the train doesn't fit the rectangular proportions of the camera frame or the video screen.

To capture a more suitable composition, move to shoot it from the front or rear.

A cutaway. While shooting a sequence of a train departing, watch for simple actions like the driver waiting for the departure time.

Another useful cutaway: checking the lamps on the front of the engine.

And another, all helping to build up the sense of imminent departure — the driver watching for the signal to change.

Advertisements, timetables, and even station signs can help to identify places or bridge gaps in the action.

able to see clearly what they are. Check the focus, and then zoom out to show the field full of cars – once again being prepared to move so that the frame at the wide end of the shot is as you want it. Then record the shot, zooming in slowly from the field full of cars, to reveal the rosette at the end of the zoom as it grows larger in the frame.

There is another way in which you can use the zoom in linking two different parts of a scene. Looking at a distant subject through the close-up end of the zoom has two very obvious effects. First, that part of the scene is foreshortened, so that objects which may be a fair distance apart, but which are even further from the camera, look as if they're very close together.

The other effect, which makes a different kind of transition shot possible, is that the depth of field of the lens (the range of distances over which objects are all in focus for a given setting) is shorter at a close-up setting of the zoom than it would be for a wide shot. So objects which may appear close together in the frame of this kind of shot may – if they're far enough apart in reality – give the game away by one object appearing in focus, and the other one being suf-ficiently out of focus to be a vague and mysterious image.

All the camera operator has to do to make the transition between one image and the other is to hold the camera very still and turn the focus ring slowly. One object will then slowly melt out of focus while the other one sharpens and becomes clear. It's a neat tech-nique, but you can only use it when the two subjects between them fill the frame, and when the difference in distance is enough to make the change-focus effect work.

Sometimes you can actually see one object through the other – a child playing seen through a set of playground railings, for example – and this makes the change-focus a specially attractive shot. But, as always with tricky shots like this, remember two things above all. Hold the camera as steadily as you can, and try the shot several times until you're pleased with the effect before you actually record it. That's another reason for picking reasonably static subjects at this stage of your experience with the camera.

So far, we've concentrated on the different types of shot, some of the transitions between them, and the ways in which you can use these transitions to create different effects. But we haven't, as yet, looked closely enough at what goes into the individual shots them-selves.

This, too, depends on what you're trying to say with your pict-ures, and in a sense your first decisions come when you try to decide what you want to shoot in the first place, and why you want to shoot it. Take a shot of someone driving a car in the vintage car rally we've just been looking at. If you want to concentrate on the driver, then you need to frame the shot so that the driver is the most important element in the shot. If the focus of interest is the car, then you need a wider framing so that the car-and-driver combination fills the frame properly.

It's possible to give a series of dont's – things to avoid in framing your shots. When you want to shoot someone talking, for example, either go for a close-up, showing the whole face with a reasonable space around it, or go for a big close-up, concentrating on the eyes and mouth if you want to put your subject under close scrutiny. Both shots have their place, and if your subject had a lot to say, you might well use both types of shot, and a medium shot, showing them as head-and-shoulders, together with a suggestion of the person they're speaking to on one edge of the frame, if you feel that helps the shot.

What you mustn't do is shoot something in between, so that the framing looks wrong. A 'talking head' with the chin resting on the bottom of the frame, or the top of the head just touching the top of the frame, looks oddly cramped. And watch out for the background.

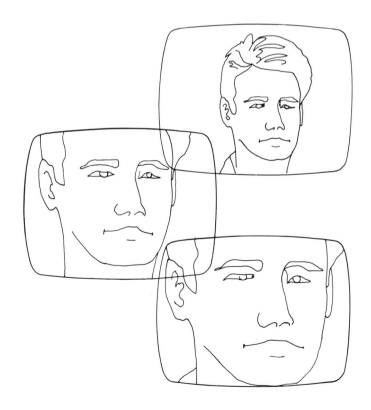

Framing faces is straightforward. Go for a close-up showing the whole face (*top*), or concentrate on the eyes and mouth (*centre*). Don't let the chin rest on the bottom of the frame, however (*bottom*), or let the top of the head just touch the top of the frame.

A change-focus shot. By adjusting the focus ring, the camera can link two subjects without moving. Here, the bars of the gateway are in focus, and the action behind them is a moving blur of colour.

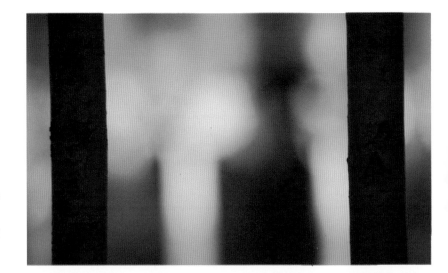

As the action changes, the bars swim out of focus . . .

And the background subject sharpens to reveal itself as a military band.

A high-angle shot. When circumstances allow, a good introductory shot of an event like a vintage car rally is to shoot it from above. Not only does it cover the whole subject well, but the elevated viewpoint enables you to avoid including a large area of sky in the picture, which can cause contrast and exposure problems.

Be on the lookout for what artists and photographers call 'rhythm'. The repetition of the lines of cars or marching men can make an interesting composition.

Choose your shot so that you emphasize rhythm as much as possible by shooting ALONG the lines of men or vehicles.

Because the picture you shoot, and the picture you see on the screen as a result, is a two-dimensional image, then someone with a telegraph pole behind them is going to look much stranger than they do in reality. Your eyes see in three dimensions, and you can appreciate how far apart they are – but on the screen, it will look as if your subject has a telegraph pole growing out of his head, or a set of overhead wires coming out of her ears. And never make it difficult to see the subject. Blocking off half the screen with the person your subject is talking to is going to be irritating; your audience will be craning their necks trying to see past them.

Framing faces is fairly straightforward. Try positioning your subject with the bridge of the nose about two-thirds of the way up the frame. If they're looking to the right (that's your right, not theirs – in other words, 'camera right') then place them on the left side of the frame. In the trade, that's called 'looking room'. It avoids them looking as if they're staring at the edge of the frame. In the same way, anyone who's walking across your field of view, if you're following them with the camera, needs to be given 'walking room', if they're not to appear to be bumping into the edge of the frame every now and again.

Because the television screen is so much smaller than the cinema screen, fine detail in a picture tends to get lost. So close-ups generally work well – which means framing your shots as tightly as possible wthout constricting them too tightly. But you can't make a programme entirely out of close-ups. Unless you have a wide shot somewhere in each sequence to establish where everything is, and put all the close-ups in context, then an endless successsion of close-ups would become claustrophobic and wearing.

Remember about the two-dimensional image. If your wide shot is of a far-off background, like a range of distant hills and a stream in the middle distance, then try to find something to fill the foreground and give the picture extra depth. If the foreground is made up of people, like a family picnic, then try and make sure some of your cast are nearer the camera, and others further back. This will add to the impression of depth, and make the shot more interesting.

There are other ideas you can use to make your shots more varied. Since we see the world from our own eye level, it seems logical to shoot from roughly that level for most of the time. But now and again you can create a different effect by shooting a subject from very low down. This can magnify the size of a person or an object, and make them look much more dominant and imposing. Or you can position yourself and the camera so you're looking down at the subject instead, which can add a sense of detachment and secrecy – almost as if the camera is eavesdropping on what is happening below.

34

In the end, you have to decide for yourself what is the main focus of interest in your picture. In a wide shot, you should try and place that focus in the centre of the frame, trying to compose the picture and choose your camera angle so that the viewer's eye is directed straight to that particular part of frame. If your audience has to wonder what the main point of interest is, then you, as the camera operator, are not doing your job properly.

There are exceptions to this rule, however. Sometimes you come across a subject which has an appeal of its own, over the whole of the frame rather than a particular focal point. A city crowd rushing from station to office may present itself through your viewfinder as a sea of faces, all walking towards you, and filling the whole of the frame. An endless succession of feet on a staircase, or even a line of repeated objects – all these shots have a visual rhythm which gives them an individual appeal, and it's worth being on the lookout for this kind of effect, wherever – and whatever – you're shooting. Even in the vintage car rally, a long line of parked cars stretching right into the distance has this magical quality of visual rhythm which makes it worth capturing on tape.

In the end, it's impossible to give a set of hard and fast rules to cover every subject, and every situation. Most of all, learning to set up, frame, and capture shots is a matter of practice, so that you know what you're looking for, and you can recognise a good subject when it stares you in the viewfinder. The more you can develop a good picture sense, and the more developed your sense of composition, the more quickly you can react to your subjects, and the more enjoyment you'll derive from your video-making.

So keep on shooting and analysing your shots – while you're rehearsing them, while you're shooting them, and while you're watching them being played back on the screen. Was your framing tight enough, without being too tight? Was the prime interest in your picture clearly and properly displayed? Did the shot do what you wanted it to do? Did you shoot a close-up when you should have used a medium shot to do the subject justice? The happier you feel with your shots, as shots, rather than as part of a planned and structured programme, the sooner you'll be able to move on to the next stage of video production: taking all the shots we've been looking at and linking them, into a properly planned and edited sequence.

As a start, have a look at the three pictures on page 41. They're deliberately chosen to say too much, to show too much, and to leave too much background in shot. Try thinking how you'd frame them, to show each of the points mentioned in the captions. Would you use a medium shot, a close-up, or a big close-up? Where would you place the edges of your frame? When you've thought about each of them carefully, compare your ideas with the answers at the back of the book. If your ideas don't tally with what we've said, don't be disheartened – there's more ways than one of shooting a subject – but try and analyse your thinking, to see if what you've suggested is equally viable.

If your answers tally with ours almost all the way through, then it could well be you're blessed with a natural sense of composition – or at the very least, we're making the same mistakes! Either way, remember to keep an eye open for the unexpected shot, the one which breaks all the rules, but which can stand out in an otherwise crowded programme as the image which really lives in the memory, when all the other carefully planned, correctly composed shots have been long forgotten. Recognising those, framing them and capturing them, often when the opportunity is only fleeting. That's what professional camera work is really all about.

TURNING OFF THE HOSEPIPE

If you look at most unskilled amateur videos, they tend to suffer from one common fault. Whatever the quality of the equipment, whatever the interest of the subject, the person operating the camera seems to be unaware of how to stop recording. One shot leads straight into another; in fact, the programme becomes a single shot for minutes on end, with the camera panning right and left and zooming in and out, and even just wobbling uncertainly from one part of the scene to another.

Sometimes you find yourself watching one subject; then, for no clearly apparent reason, the camera's attention wanders to a different subject, then back to the first one. Sometimes in the middle of a move from one subject to another, the camera operator will have second thoughts, and swing back to the first subject again. The camera movements resemble someone using a hose to water a lawn, wash a car, or put out a small fire: they wander restlessly backwards and forwards, until the whole area has been thoroughly soaked.

No wonder this approach to shooting is often called 'hosepipe direction', and it's the clearest giveaway of all that the person behind the camera has no very clear idea of what he or she is doing. They're simply reacting to the subject, rather than imposing their own plans, ideas, and objectives on the material they are trying to record. And the result is that the recording is tiring, distracting, and boring to watch – quite literally, a waste of time and tape.

So the next step in producing a professional home video is to learn the value of discipline. This operates in two ways. It means deciding very firmly what each shot is FOR. What should you be looking at, and why? What subjects are you trying to link together? What effects are you trying to create? How does a particular shot relate to the previous shot, and how will it relate to its successor? When you have thought about all these matters, and decided exactly what you want the shot to achieve, then you will have fixed what kind of shot it should be. You'll have fixed where it should start, where it should finish, and more or less how long it should last. All you have to do is rehearse the shot, modify it wherever you feel it might be improved, and then record it.

The discipline comes in sticking precisely to the plan you have worked out in your head and rehearsed beforehand. Don't change your mind in mid-shot. If you have a sudden flash of inspiration, or if some change in the subject opens up another, better possibility, finish your shot first. Only then decide whether or not it's worth replacing it with a different version, or whether your first idea was better after all. It may well be that you can have the best of both worlds, and think of another view of the subject which follows logically after the shot you have just recorded. We'll look at how to build up a sequence of shots later. In the meantime there's the second aspect of self-discipline to consider, and the hardware which will help you to achieve it.

It's all to do with keeping a steady picture. Even if careful planning and a refusal to be diverted from that plan does manage to avoid the worst outbreaks of the hosepipe effect, it's still essential to hold the camera as steadily as possible while you're recording. This too takes practice. Even for a skilled and experienced cameraman, keeping the camera still during a long and difficult zoom is a very difficult proposition.

It's even worse if you need to keep looking at something on the close-up end of the zoom for a long time, since every movement of the camera will seem magnified when you watch the shot on playback afterwards. So it's essential to think in terms of a tripod, to support the camera for you, and to help you with the more difficult transition shots. In fact, it's fair to say that next to your camera and recorder, the tripod is possibly the the most important item of video equipment.

If you're using a tripod with an ordinary stills camera, then it has a fairly simple job to do – to hold your camera steady for the duration of the exposure, which even in very low light isn't likely to be more than a minute at the most. This type of tripod may be suitable for use with a video camera, too, if your main purpose is to find a camera platform for static shots, or the kind of absolutely standard zooms in and out, where the camera doesn't move at all – the lens system, and the subject, does all the moving for you.

But this is only part of what a tripod should be capable of, in making a movie programme. Take a close look at any feature film or television documentary, and you'll find the camera is on the move for a great deal of the time. Apart from panning and tilting shots, there are combinations of pans and tilts and zooms to cover a complex transition from one subject to another, which would need a great deal of experience (and quite a few attempts) to get right with a shoulder-supported camera.

So can a tripod help? Yes, if it's the right type of tripod, or if you know what its limitations are. All camera tripods will have a mounting platform for the camera, which can be panned and tilted so that you can aim the camera at the subject, wherever it is. There will also be a pair of locking wheels or butterfly nuts which allow you to fix the camera at the desired angle. This is fine for static shots, but the locks need to be loosened for anything where the camera itself has to move. And this is where the problems start. When you start to pan, for example, you have to overcome any friction within the tripod before the camera platform begins to pivot. But because static friction is greater than rolling friction, once you've overcome that resistance you suddenly need less force to keep the camera panning.

What this means in practice is that the pan often starts with a perceptible jerk, as the platform suddenly starts to move. The pan may then be steady enough, but as you slow down at the end of the pan, the frictional resistance of the tripod head will suddenly re-assert itself, and the pan will stop with another perceptible snatch. To solve this problem, professional tripods often have heavy, fluid-mounted heads which smooth out these start-stop transitions as far as possible, and make the movement as smooth as possible. But they're heavy, cumbersome and expensive, so the chances are you'll have to manage with a tripod less well suited to the job in hand.

What's the answer? Once again, it's all down to practice. The more you can accustom yourself to the amount of effort needed to start and stop a pan or a tilt smoothly, and the right amount of friction you need to set with the locking adjustments on the tripod head to make this possible, the better your shots will be. But make sure the tripod itself is heavy enough for the job. When you WANT a static camera position, is the tripod strong enough to support the camera securely? Or does it shudder under every gust of wind, so that close-ups become difficult to do, even with the tripod to help you?

Tripods do need to be used carefully. If you plan to record a shot which involves panning and tilting, then you will have to loosen both adjustments to make it possible to move the head smoothly. But when your shot is finished, make sure you lock the camera platform securely. Otherwise, as soon as you let go of the tripod handle, the weight of the camera will tilt it forward or backwards quite sharply, depending on the positioning of the tripod mounting and the camera's own centre of gravity. Either way, you could easily damage the camera – and if it tilts backwards, the lens could point directly at the sun, causing internal damage if fitted with tubes.

There are two other problems worth bearing in mind when you're using a tripod. One is that you may well find, when you're panning to follow a moving object, that the object may also move up or down when you're not expecting it to, so you could find it vanishing through the top or bottom of your frame. And the other problem is that tripods themselves could have been designed for people to trip over their outstretched legs. Watch that no-one ruins your shot by catching a tripod leg at the wrong moment – at the very least, you'll have a spoiled shot. At the worst, you could damage the camera or cause an injury to someone by unintentionally tripping them up. And that includes you. When you're concentrating hard on what you're seeing through the viewfinder in a difficult pan, it's all too easy to trip over your own tripod legs.

In buying a tripod, it's wise to look for the very best you can afford. One day, you may want to exchange your camera for a more professional one or a more versatile one, but a good tripod will always stand you in good stead. And the more features it carries, the more it will improve your shooting, whatever the quality of the camera you may be using, either now, or in the future.

A lightweight tripod (*top left*) with an adjustable head, known as a pan-and-tilt head, which can pan, tilt or swing the camera from side to side.

Cheap friction heads (*top right*) with no cushioning between the plates, tend to be jerky. Moving from pan to tilt entails loosening both controls while supporting the camera.

This camera (*bottom*) is fitted to a sophisticated tripod mounted on a set of wheels, or dollies, which may be collapsible, and fitted with brakes, direction locks and guards to lift stray cables.

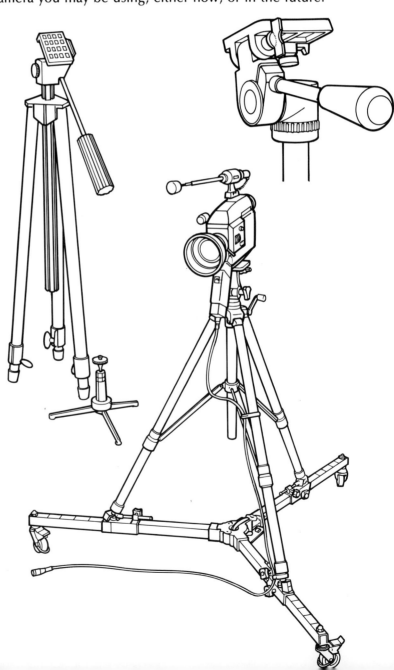

Half the battle in producing interesting pictures is to frame them correctly. Here are three wide shots of different subjects.

Look carefully at all three, and decide how you would frame close-ups from each.

Which is the real centre of interest in each picture?

What kind of features should the ideal tripod have? A fluid-mounted head, if you can afford one, since this will make the most difference to the smoothness and professionalism of your shooting. Strong construction – video cameras are now considerably lighter than cine-cameras, but you want a tripod which is not only going to support your camera without the threat of failure, but is going to provide a STEADY mounting for your moving shots. A good range of adjustment of the tripod legs is a worthwhile feature – extendible legs allow you to shoot from a viewpoint higher than eye level, if you can find a suitable box to stand on to reach the camera controls. And legs which can be splayed out to an almost horizontal position give you the option of the occasional low-level shot when holding the camera steady without the tripod might be difficult, or even impossible.

Another useful feature is a spirit-level on the tripod mounting. If you're setting up for a pan with the background in shot, then you want the camera to be level all the way round the pan. One way of doing this is to set the tripod up, and then to pan the camera round while checking that the horizon remains level all the way round. But this can be a cumbersome and time-consuming business: it's far easier to check with a built-in spirit-level that everything is level before you start.

Some tripods can even be fitted with a set of wheels. This gives you the option of yet another shot – the tracking shot – where the camera and tripod move bodily while shooting, either to follow a moving subject backwards, forwards or sideways, or whether to bring a different perspective to a scene by moving the camera through it.

Successful tracking shots depend on a number of factors – among them the smoothness of the surface over which the tripod wheels will be tracking – but once again, practice makes perfect. The start of the shot, when the camera moves from the static position to the start of its tracking movement, and the end, where it comes to a stop again, are the most difficult parts of a tracking shot to get right. But if these difficulties can be overcome, there are some striking effects which a good tracking shot can capture, which make it worth bearing in mind as a worthwhile objective.

Are there any alternatives to a tripod, if a good one is too expensive, or if you don't have one with you? The most distracting camera movement is usually the up-and-down one. If you can keep the camera steady in the horizontal plane, then achieving steady shots, and steady pans, is much easier. So a simple camera support, leaving you to make these movements by hand, can be a worthwhile alternative to completely hand-held operation. You can opt for the kind of monopod – a single, telescopic leg with a camera mounting at the top – which stills cameramen use, as a viable alternative to the tripod in some cases. Pans will be easier than they will be without any extra support, and there's no inherent frictional problems as there would be with the cheaper and simpler tripod heads. It's also easier to follow a moving subject and cater for any unexpected dips or swoops by tilting the leg of the monopod backwards or forwards enough to keep the subject in the frame. The monopod is also lighter than any worthwhile tripod, and worth bearing in mind whenever the subject-matter means that portability and speed of movement from place to place are important requirements.

Various ways of achieving camera stability. They range from using a wall as a support to strong elastic secured around the foot or to the belt or an improvised monopod. However, it is always best to use a proper support. No improvisation can really beat a tripod or a monopod.

If even a monopod is out of the question on a particular shoot, then keep an eye open for any source of support at all. You can steady a shot by finding a convenient wall to lean on – either a horizontal surface to support your arms, and the camera, or a vertical wall against which you can lean bodily while concentrating on steadying the camera. And there's even a dodge which is worth bearing in mind for tracking shots without tripods. If you can find any kind of transport, from a supermarket trolley to a wheelchair, get someone to push you through the tracking movement, while you sit in the chair and cradle the camera as steadily as you can. With a little bit of practice on your part, and that of the person pushing you, the results can be surprisingly effective.

Once you've practised these different types of shot, with whatever equipment you're able to lay your hands on, let's now turn to look at how shots can be linked together to make a sequence on a particular subject. At this stage, we will assume that you are effectively editing in the machine which you're using to record. In other words, the order in which you shoot the shots will be the order in which they will appear in the finished sequence. This means thinking very carefully about each shot in turn, but there's no reason why the finished sequence need not be as polished and professional as if you were able to edit and reshuffle and select from the material afterwards, as a professional production team would be able to do.

On the other hand, the more sophisticated cameras can be used in combination with your domestic video recorder (depending on its type) to edit together a finished programme just like the professional programme-makers do it. Essentially, it works like this: the camera is plugged into the VCR, which is loaded with a blank cassette and set to record in the ordinary way. But by using the camera as a playback machine, and setting the controls to pick the individual shots you want, you can build up a complete programme on the new cassette in the VCR. You can pick the shots you want from any number of tapes, and then copy them from the camera one by one.

There are certain principles which apply to whatever subject you choose for your first sequence. Going back to the earlier examples of a preserved railway, or a vintage car rally, they both satisfy two requirements as programme subjects. They're full of colour, and they're full of movement. Generally speaking, television – or video – doesn't treat static subjects well at all. The medium lacks the quality, in terms of sharpness and clarity, which top-quality photographs and slides can capture. So where a subject is static by its nature, then it often calls for a top-quality presenter to lend it the interest and movement it would otherwise lack. Kenneth Clark's series 'Civilisation' was a good example of this way of bringing static subjects like buildings or paintings to life in an imaginative and entertaining way.

As a general rule, though, be on the lookout for change, as well as movement. To take the railway example, the departure of the train makes a far better sequence than the station during a period when nothing is happening. During the vintage car rally, try to concentrate on a moment when something definite is going on. Either the cars might be arriving and are being marshalled into orderly lines in the car-park, or the judges are walking around checking which ones are worthy of being awarded prizes – or the prizes themselves are actually being handed over to the winners. It isn't a bad idea to note whether all the other people on the scene are watching you, or whether they're looking at whatever it is you're shooting. If they're all looking at you, then it's fairly certain that your subject isn't interesting enough on its own. Look for something which is successful in distracting everyone's attention from you and your camera. At the very least, it will mean less of the waving hands and stares into the camera which can ruin the best-planned shots at the worst possible moment.

Having found a good subject, where there's plenty of action and interest, try to plan how you'll capture it with the camera. It's easier to cope with action which is continuing, or which is predictable, than something which happens quickly and with little warning. For example, a race where cars are going round and round a track gives you time to shoot your sequence in whatever order you like – the timed departure, or arrival of a train gives you something to work towards in building up your sequence. A sudden passing car, or a low-flying aeroplane, may be a dramatic event, but you won't have the time or the warning to do it justice.

Where things are under your control, try to start with a general shot to establish your subject properly. In the case of the railway example, it would be the station platform, with the waiting train and the crowd of spectators. You could then cut to some of the details in the scene to bring them into greater prominence. What about the smoke coming from the engine's funnel, or the driver and fireman sharing a cup of tea on the footplate, or a small boy looking with fascination at the hissing steel monster? You could zoom in to one of these – but you would then have to cut from one to another to build up the sequence. And don't be afraid to move your camera position in between shots, to give a different perspective on the scene from time to time.

You can always include the odd static subject, provided it's kept brief, and provided it has a place in the sequence. For example, the nameboard of the station to identify the location – or a departure board, showing the time and destination of the train, to identify the event we're waiting for – act as graphics in telling part of the story for you. Generally speaking, you need to keep these shots running for as long as it takes people to read the name, or the information, twice, very slowly. This is because the audience has to have time to react before they can start absorbing the information.

If your general shot and your close-ups have worked so far, you can now try to build up a second sequence of a particular activity going on. And this is where you need to bear two more factors in mind: continuity and cutaways.

Let's say, for example, that you want to shoot the stationmaster coming out of his office to have a word with the driver on the footplate. If you shoot him coming out of his office door, you could then follow him all the way along the platform to the engine, and end on the two men in conversation. But that might mean a shot which is on the screen far too long for the interest it carries for the audience. So how can you shorten it?

One option might be to shoot the stationmaster emerging from his office, and closing the door behind him. If you then stop the camera, follow him further down the platform and then start re-cording when he's almost at the engine, the chances are you will be up against that eternal problem which faces anyone trying to com-press time by being selective in what they shoot: the jump-cut.

Because the surroundings are much the same in the second shot as they are in the first, then all the audience is conscious of is that the stationmaster has suddenly made a jump from one end of the platform to another. There are times when you can make use of this effect, but they're limited to special circumstances. In most cases, producing a professional video means avoiding jump-cuts like the plague. But how can you do this without showing the stationmaster's walk in its entirety, or having to leave out the shot which might have an important role in the sequence?

There are two ways to solve this problem. One is to fit another shot in between the stationmaster leaving his office and his arrival at the engine. It doesn't even need to take up the time which he would have taken from one place to the other. Because it involves a look at an entirely different subject, the audience won't notice the speed with which the stationmaster manages to move from one end of the platform to the other. But make sure that your cutaway is one which doesn't show the platform – otherwise he will seem to disappear from outside his office, and reappear at the engine. If, for example, you include a shot of a timetable, or of the signalman looking out through the signalbox window, then in your next shot you can show the stationmaster arriving at the engine to talk to the driver. What you've done is use a cutaway shot to bridge what would otherwise have been a jump-cut.

The other solution is to change the camera position to disguise the jump-cut, without having to use a cutaway. If your shot of the stationmaster leaving his office is recorded with your back to the engine, then the audience won't be aware of the distance between the two places. If your next shot is framed fairly tightly on the engine cab, the stationmaster can walk into the frame when he's completed his walk down the platform, without the audience being aware, even at this stage, of how long that walk should have taken. It's possible to overdo the effect, so that the action is still shortened too much to be credible – but the rule is that if it looks right, then it IS right. And it's a good idea always to be on the lookout for ways of shortening shots which might otherwise be boring, by stopping the camera and moving to a new viewpoint. That way, your programme will have a faster pace, it will be more entertaining, and your audience will be less likely to find their attention wandering.

It's always wise to bear these objectives in mind ALL the time. Remind yourself always to be on the lookout for the unexpected, the interesting, and the unusual. Sometimes it's worth making your audience sit up and wonder what it is about a shot which lends it a slightly different quality. Instead of simply including a shot of the signalbox as a cutaway to the action, try shooting it through the smoke coming from the engine's funnel, so it appears as a mist-shrouded image, swimming in and out of view. Or shoot it through the waves of heat coming up from the footplate and the firebox, so it shimmers like a mirage.

Reflections are another useful source of unusual shots. Try shooting a signal, or a set of faces, reflected in a pool of water, or the polished brass and copper work on the engine. They will look distorted, and they'll change as they move in a confusing way. Once the shot has lasted long enough for the audience to wonder what's happening, then you can pull back to show enough of the surroundings to set the shot in its context. They'll see, and understand, what was confusing and intriguing in close-up, and it will be another focus of interest in the middle of an otherwise straightforward sequence. But – as with any other special effect – beware of overdoing it. Too many distorted and confusing shots can be as distracting to watch as a sequence of entirely straightforward and predictable images. Use these shots sparingly, to maximise their effect and maintain the interest as much as possible. If you have a full edit facility (refer to page 13), then you are free to experiment with these more unusual types of shot without worrying about whether each one is successful, or whether they are upsetting the overall balance of the material, since you will be selecting the shots to be used in the finished programme at the editing stage. So you can shoot as many ideas as you like – with this kind of flexibility at your disposal, it is far better to have too many ideas to choose from, than too few.

Finally, try these techniques out on as many different subjects as possible. Each one demands a different plan, a different way of thinking. The varied experience you're building up will prove to be priceless later on, with more ambitious and more specific aims in mind. Review your work critically. Be on the lookout for mistakes and areas which could be improved, and in time you'll see your own work improving before your eyes – the best encouragement of all.

How to avoid the dreaded jump-cut. The porter is walking towards you, but is going to take too long to reach the front of the train. How do you speed up the action without a jump-cut?

Simply cut to a different angle to show the porter arriving at his destination, and you can disguise the fact that you've lost part of the intervening walk.

Another cutaway: children on a tank at a military band concert. But shooting against the light tends to produce a silhouette effect, so be careful how you use this kind of shot.

LET THERE BE LIGHT

Chapter 4

So far we have concentrated on outdoor shooting, where the light is usually bright enough to obtain good pictures without having to take extra trouble. Even so, some factors will already have made themselves obvious. The best pictures are usually shot with the main source of light – the sun – falling evenly on the scene at which you're aiming the camera. And as video cameras tend to be unhappy with subjects with very high contrast between light and shade, those results will be best with the sun behind you, cutting the areas of deep shadow to the minimum.

This means that shooting into the sun is to be avoided as much as possible. Apart from the danger of possible damage to some of the older types of camera which would result from letting direct sunlight in through the lens, all the parameters are wrong. Your subject – or the side of it turned towards you – would be in shadow, and you would be seeing it against the brightness of direct sunlight. This must be the harshest contrast you can imagine, and the picture you get will vary between an overbright background, and a subject which will be a black silhouette, if you're lucky. Depending on the actual conditions, and the quality of your camera, you might encounter problems like flaring and misting – the bright picture areas may actually appear to eat into the dark silhouette of the subject, producing distortions and smeared edges every time the camera moves slightly. So try to avoid shooting into the sun, unless it's under very controlled conditions, with a particular objective in mind.

The same is true, to a slightly lesser extent, on an overcast day with no sign of the sun at all. On a day which is grey and overcast, the sky is surprisingly bright, and the scene you're shooting will be appreciably darker because the light which falls on it from the cloud is less bright than it would be in sunlight. So the contrast you must avoid here is between the darkness or relative darkness of your subject, and the brightness of the sky. Compose your pictures with too wide a sweep of sky in the frame, and you'll find your subject becomes a dark silhouette. And while that may be fine for certain dramatic effects, it limits the story you can tell with too many images like that in a sequence.

So is the best way to shoot a picture to choose a bright, sunny day, and to choose a camera position out of doors with the sun at your back? Yes, but only up to a point. Because this avoids deep pools of shadow, then a wide shot, like a landscape, is going to look very flat and two-dimensional. It also restricts your camera positions, which makes it difficult to shoot different parts of a scene from different angles, as we did in earlier chapters. And finally, because the light falls evenly over the whole scene, it isn't going to help you or the audience to pick out the main focus of interest in the picture.

What can we do about it? The answer is, partly, the art of compromise. Try working as far as possible with the sun behind the camera, but not necessarily directly behind the camera. Whenever you have a wide shot to capture, try and position yourself with the sun over one shoulder, or even to one side of you, if the shape and appearance of the subject helps you to keep the ratio between the brightly-lit areas and the patches of deep shade as favourable as possible. On sunless, overcast days, keep wide shots to the minimum, and choose viewpoints and angles which keep the area of sky in the frame to the minimum. Tall buildings or high hills all help – but if the horizon is flat, then keep it as far up the frame as possible with the framing which seems to do the subject justice.

All this has been under the assumption that weather, and lighting conditions are ideal. But sunny, cloudless days are rare in Britain, and many other countries for that matter. One reason why the American film industry soon moved to California was the plentiful sunshine of the West Coast, which was a vital requirement before indoor studios came into fashion. And the light can vary from hour to hour throughout the day, in intensity and in temperature. Just after dawn or just before sunset, the light is not only fainter than it is at midday, it also has a much redder cast. Unless you make a point of looking for this effect, you may never really have noticed it, because the human eye has such a sophisticated compensating mechanism. We can react to variations in light intensity and colour temperature which a camera can't cope with without careful readjustments, and sometimes not even then.

Because of this, you have to be on the lookout for these factors whenever you might be shooting in changing circumstances. Shooting a sequence in late afternoon might be spread over an hour or two. You might not notice the difference in the light during that time, but the camera almost certainly will. The result is that shots at the end of the sequence will look as if they're shot in a warmer, lower light than the human eye will be aware of – it will look an hour or two later on the screen, than the surroundings appear in real life. And unless it suits your purpose to hint in the sequence that twilight is closing in, the effect can be quite distracting.

A similar effect occurs when you want to shoot indoors, though for different reasons. There the light which illuminates your subject will be artificial – in most cases from domestic light-bulbs, which use tungsten filaments. This means the light will have a yellow cast compared with daylight at midday, which has a distinctly blue tinge – to the camera, if not the human eye. So, if your camera is not fitted with automatic white balance, you have to remember to take these factors into account. Whenever the light is likely to change, out of doors, carry out the white-balance procedure over again. If your sequence moves from the garden into the house, stop and rebalance the camera in the indoor lighting conditions before shooting any material indoors. And if you move outside again, then rebalance the camera again before shooting.

Colour temperature is the first of the problems presented by shooting indoors – and with modern cameras, fitted with clever and easily-operated white-balance systems, it's much less of a problem than it used to be. Provided you remember to make the appropriate adjustments whenever the colour temperature changes, or is likely to change, then you should encounter no problems. But the second shortcoming of indoor shooting – the intensity of the light – isn't so easy to solve.

Once again, it's a case of the human eye being a great deal cleverer and more efficient than even the best camera. We can come indoors on a bright sunny day, and in a matter of minutes our eyes can readjust to work quite comfortably in subdued lighting. We can see our surroundings, we can read a book, we can carry on a conversation, and generally feel as relaxed and at home as we would out of doors at midday in bright sunshine. But lighting we would regard as comfortably adequate for all these purposes would be hopelessly insufficient for a camera to do the scene justice. As a rough rule of thumb, looking at an indoor scene through half-closed eyes will give you an idea of how the video camera will see it. It will pick out the pool of light cast by a standard lamp or a wall-light, and perhaps the glow of the fire, but all the other tones of the room will sink back into the background darkness. Here again, the newer cameras have greatly improved capability – some of them can produce a recognisable picture even by candlelight. But the basic principles still hold good – the brighter your lighting, the clearer and sharper your picture. And good lighting means your camera will respond better to moving subjects, and you can use the lighting to help you create the particular effects you want for the programme you are making.

So lighting an indoor location for shooting a scene with a video camera means making it much brighter than normal. But this has to be done carefully, or the extra lighting can easily do more harm than good. So let's begin by looking at the kinds of lights which can be brought into play, and then see how they should be deployed, to give the kind of results we need.

First of all, it's worth bearing in mind that ordinary domestic lighting can be boosted by fitting more powerful bulbs to the kind of directional lamps which allow you to arrange the lighting as you want it. Spotlights on stands, or on overhead tracks, or swivelling desk lamps can make ideal impromptu video lights, but you have to be careful in two areas. Some lamps have a limit on the power of the bulbs you can use in them, because of the potential danger of overheating. In any case, it's a good idea to save power as much as possible by switching them off whenever you're not shooting.

The other point you need to remember is to keep the colour temperature as constant as you can. Shooting in a kitchen with overhead fluorescent lights will provide a bluer cast, closer to daylight than artificial light. Adding tungsten bulbs as spotlights will only produce patches of yellower light, which add to the complication of producing a set of lifelike pictures through the camera, particularly when the mixture of spotlights and overhead might may vary in individual close-up shots.

The linear-type quartz halogen (*left*) gives a high-output wide beam.

Quartz lights (*right*) are economical, lightweight and universally popular.

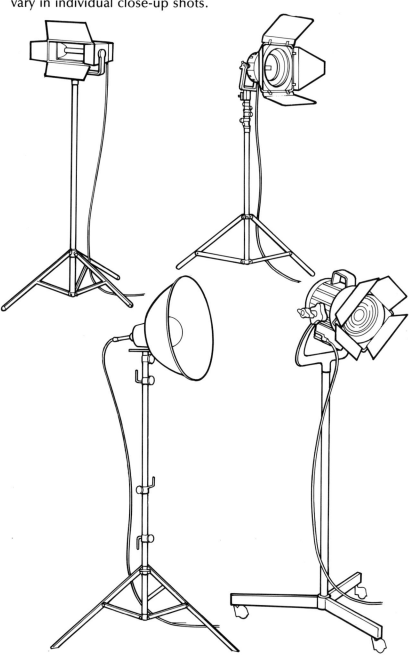

The cheap photoflood (*left*) gives a wide angle of overall illumination.

This fresnel spotlight (*right*) is mounted on a dolly. A fresnel lens can be mounted in front of a light to focus the beam, or to soften the edges of a spot.

Coloured Filters can be used to create special effects.

Here a more subtle effect has been achieved to create an atmospheric sky (courtesy *Camcorder User*).

Perhaps the best compromise, to begin with, is to improvise two lights through fitting stronger bulbs to domestic spotlights or desk lights, and using a proper photoflood or, preferably, a video light with directional baffles (known in the trade as 'barn doors') and a control which allows you to vary the beam in between a small spot of concentrated light and a wider flood of light, as your main light source. This gives you enough lights to light a single subject properly, and to show the principles of studio lighting which can be followed through to much more complex and ambitious subjects.

Now let's try lighting a simple subject: a head-and-shoulders shot of a presenter or an interviewee, for example, composed as a conventional portrait. Ask your subject to sit in a chair and stay as still as possible without discomfort, while you arrange your lighting. First, take your main light, and arrange it beside the camera, and pointing at the subject. Connect the camera, following the instructions in the operator's manual, so that you can see the picture on the screen of your television set, at full size and in full colour. Switch on the light and the camera, then hold a white card or some other suitable object in front of your subject's face and operate the white-balance adjustment. Remove the card and compose the picture, and then look at the image on the screen. You'll find that your subject's face looks flat and two-dimensional, with all the shadows and details washed out, and with a slightly disembodied feeling, as it floats in front of a large pool of shadow cast on the wall behind.

Now try moving the light away from the camera – still pointing it carefully at the subject – and check the effects of each move on the picture showing on the screen. As the light moves away from the camera at a wider angle, the features of the face will appear more and more three-dimensional, as the shadows cast by nose and eyebrows become more marked, and the shadow on the wall behind the subject will disappear to one side. If you ask your subject to look to the side of the camera on which you've placed the light – as they would in a studio interview, for example – you can avoid the shadow cast by the nose being too prominent, while still producing the three-dimensional effect of a real face rather than a flat photograph. In the same way, changing the height of the lamp can reduce the shadows cast by the eyebrows over the eye-sockets, which might otherwise look too dark and mysterious.

When the light is in the right position you will find a very powerful image on the screen, with one half of the face (or thereabouts) brilliantly lit, and the other half in deep shadow. This is the kind of dramatic effect – called chiaroscuro, from the Italian for 'bright-dark' – exploited by many of the world's greatest painters. The problem, for our purposes, is that it's a shade TOO dramatic – fine for a scene from a horror movie or a murder mystery, or a shot at a moment of tension in a play. But for a normal interview we need a second light to soften the contrast between the areas of light and dark in the face, to bring it closer to what our own eyes would see.

As a comparison, look directly at your subject's face. You will see the bright areas clearly enough, but unless the light is too bright for its job, you'll also see the shadowed portions of the face in some detail. Less bright perhaps, but not as black as the picture on the screen, which is limited by the range of contrast which the camera can cope with. So once again, we have to use a light to make the camera's job – of standing in for the human eye – a little bit easier, and a great deal more possible.

The first light is called the key light, the second light is called the filler, which describes its job fairly well. It needs to be placed where it can fill in those areas of shadow and hint at the substance of the face – what it must NOT do is rival the intensity of the key light, or we would regress to the beginning, with a flat, two-dimensional face with even illumination all over and no hint of the detail which gives it depth and helps it to come alive.

This means that while the key light has to be a hard light, the filler light must be softer. In other words, it must throw a more diffused beam which will provide a soft illumination to the shadowed side of the face, without casting more hard shadows of its own. Because natural light tends to cast shadows in one main direction, lighting your subject with two or more hard lights would produce a jumble of conflicting shadows which would create a confusing picture.

So place your filler light – a soft photoflood, perhaps, for best results – on the opposite side of the camera from your key light; and adjust its beam so as to lift the light level on the shadowed side of the face, so that you can see enough detail on the screened image. Once again, move the light backwards and forwards, and adjust its height up and down to produce the best combination.

Now you have two of your lights in place, look again at the picture on the screen, and compare it with the view you have when looking directly at your subject. The biggest difference of which you should still be conscious will be in the relationship of the subject to the background. In reality, you can see the wall behind your subject's head well enough, in the light scattered from the rest of the room. On the screen, the background will either tend to vanish into darkness, in the contrast with the fully-lit face, or it may be partly illuminated by light thrown from the key and filler lights. Either way, it will present a distraction, one which can only be eliminated by adding some extra illumination to lift the background to the kind of level perceived by the eye.

This is done by the third light in the basic lighting kit: the backlight. Like the keylight, this should be another hard light, but it should be angled to miss the subject altogether, apart from casting an extra sparkle on his or her hair to help the subject stand out from the background. But this effect should be left to the very edge of the area of light cast by the back-light. The main target is the background itself. Too much light cast on to the subject would weaken this effect, and perhaps create more confusing shadows to spoil the effect already created around the subject's face. You can try different places for the backlight, but you will probably find the best effects can be produced by having it on the same side of the subject as the keylight, but slightly behind the subject rather than in front of him or her.

Area lighting. Lamps positioned like this allow actors to move around on the set and still remain effectively lit.

The backlight completes the basic lighting arrangement for a single subject, though it's clear that this is a complete simplification of the kind of lighting needed for most scenes. For example, if you were shooting an interview or conversation between two people, then in theory each one would need three lights to achieve this kind of properly-lit, three-dimensional effect. In these circumstances, you could light each shot separately, moving the lights whenever the conversation shifts from one to the other. This would produce ideal conditions, at the expense of losing all spontaneity from the interview and stretching out the time taken to shoot it to an impossible extent. Better to accept a compromise and light the scene as a whole, with one subject's keylight arranged to scatter enough light on to the other subject to act as a filler, and a single backlight to cover the background to both. But each extra person, or each extra focus of interest, will add another requirement to the lighting setup – and that's without worrying about the effects of any of the people in the scene actually getting up and walking about!

Let's now look at the factors which have to be taken into account in lighting an indoor scene. In this case, the job is more complicated than the fairly simple task of creating an even background for the faces of your subjects. If you have a living room which you want to use as scenery for a conversation, or an event like a record of a family party, for example, then the effect you need to produce is the existing lighting present in the room, but intensified to the level where the video camera can do justice to the scene when it finally appears on the television screen.

It's slightly easier if we look at creating an evening scene first, where all the lighting is artificial, and daylight doesn't need to be taken into account. Try looking at the scene through half-closed eyes, to see it as the camera will see it – or switch the camera on, and watch the result on the television screen to see EXACTLY what the camera is recording. You will be most aware of the existing lights – a standard lamp behind the sofa perhaps, a wall-light to the right of the door, a table lamp beside the fireplace. Next, look for the areas where the light cast from these different sources illuminates the floor, the furniture, or the walls. This is the picture you will have to create as accurately as possible, while lifting the light intensity to the point where the camera will see things as your eyes do when looking into the room.

Begin by trying to intensify your light sources. If the bulbs themselves can't be seen by the camera, because of the angles of the lampshades or the directional spotlights, then you can fit stronger bulbs to intensify the light they cast on the surroundings. Another way of increasing the light thrown on the floor and the walls is to use more lights, aimed at the right parts of the background, but hidden from the camera by being out of the shooting area, or concealed behind the furniture. You can make the most of the lights you have by using reflectors. Professional film-makers often use sheets of reflective material when shooting out of doors in bright sunlight, to reflect the sunshine on to the shadowed side of a face and act as a filler. And you can create the same effects indoors to throw soft pools of light on to walls or furniture or even ceilings, to create the right effect.

Reflectors can be bought from specialist photographic suppliers: but you can always make your own. All you need is a sheet of plywood, or thick cardboard and a roll of kitchen cooking foil. If you glue a flat sheet of foil on one side of the wood or card, you have a reflective surface which can directly reflect a hard light over a limited area. If you now crumple a second sheet of foil slightly to produce a more diffuse reflection, and glue that to the other side of the wood or cardboard, you now have a reflector sheet which can act as a back-up spot or floodlight, depending on which side you use to reflect the light – and two or three reflector boards will increase your options in lighting a scene properly.

Another factor which needs considering is the kind of mood you want to establish. If the overall light level is still on the dark and subdued side, rather like a shot of someone staring into a glowing fire, lost in thought with only a few lights scattered in the background, then the mood the scene will create in the minds of the audience will tend to be subdued and reflective too. For a party, though, you'd expect a brighter scene altogether, to emphasise the gaiety and animation of the event, so you would need to take the extra trouble to make the picture as bright as possible with the resources you have available. In each case, you are making the lighting work for you, in creating the mood you want the scene to portray.

What happens, though, when you want to create an indoor scene in the daytime? You still need to lift the light level indoors to the point where the camera is able to make it look lifelike, but unless you're able to afford special daylight-type filming lights, you're going to have to create this effect with yellowish artificial light, which doesn't mix well with real daylight. How can we solve this problem without mixing colour temperatures?

There are two answers to this question, both of them involving making sure all the light is effectively at the same colour temperature. If you want to suggest broad daylight, aided by just a little artificial light in the corners of the room, then you can turn your yellowish artificial lights into a bluer daylight cast by screening them with blue filters. These are sheets of blue gel which can be hung in front of the lights, or which can be clipped to the 'barn-doors' of video lights, using bulldog clips. The result will be a scene which looks as if it's lit predominantly by daylight, and you may need to heighten the effect of the light streaming in through the window – to make up for lifting the light level WITHIN the room – by putting an extra light or two outside the window, pointing inwards. Since these too are likely to be yellowish in the light they throw, you'll need to screen them with sheets of blue gel, either individually or spread over the whole window-pane.

If, on the other hand, you need to suggest morning or evening light, then the yellowish cast of your artificial light is less of a problem. You can leave your interior lights alone, but the real daylight coming in through the window may be more difficult to eliminate. So this time, you need a sheet of orange-yellow gel to fit over the window pane, and then if you need to boost the light coming in from the window, you can still add a light or two without needing to correct their temperature any further.

It may sound a dauntingly complex business, but it's a vital part of every professional television production, and good lighting, carefully laid out, will make a spectacular difference to the pictures you can record at home, or at work. As you grow more ambitious, you may even find you want to spend a little more money on more powerful lighting, as you can very rarely have too MUCH lighting available for when you need it. For example, one drawback of the use of filters to even out the colour temperature in mixed daylight-artificial-light combinations is that they work by subtracting some of the light your lamps are producing. So, as always, the need is likely to be for light, and more light, and yet more light.

On the other hand, lighting has to be planned and used with care. When shooting outside, you have light which tends to be even, except when you're placed in shadows cast by buildings or the landscape. But when shooting indoors, you need to use the lighting as an extra ally to help make sure your audience's attention is focussed fairly and squarely on what you want them to concentrate on. It's no good putting your subject – presenter, interviewee, or whatever – in subdued lighting next to part of the scenery which is brilliantly illuminated, like a sofa or a pot plant. If you do, they will focus immediately on the pot plant or the sofa, and when the subject moves or speaks, it will be a distraction, instead of a clear and logical part of the action.

So this introduces yet another factor into your lighting plan. You have to light for mood, you have to light for effect, in making the scene look lifelike for morning, evening, twilight or midday; and you have to light to concentrate on the main areas of interest in each of your shots. Sometimes these may seem to be impossible objectives to reach in the same scene, but careful compromise will solve most problems. If the lighting plan works well, but your subjects are in the wrong place for the best effect, try moving them, or moving the furniture on which they sit, or through which they move. And movement is yet another potential problem which must be borne in mind.

Imagine you have a room, perfectly lit for where you want your subjects to sit – but you want one of them to enter through a door, walk into the room and sit down. You will need to check the effect of that movement on your scene. Can you see through the open door as your subject enters, through to a dark hallway which seems pitch-black compared with your well-lit room? Then you will need a filler light in the hallway to make it look as if it's at least partially lit – or you need to move the camera slightly or change the framing of the shot, or the way your subject comes through the door, so that you DON'T see the hallway beyond. Now check the walk through the room – does the movement cast any confusing or unwanted shadows on the other people already present? If so, you may be able to solve the problem with an extra light or two (remember, you can NEVER have too many lights), or by shooting the entrance into the room as two separate shots, or by changing the route of your subject's walk.

Silhouetting can produce dramatic effects.

Don't be afraid to fill the viewer with large areas of bright colour.

Special filtering creates the star-shaped flash of sunlight (courtesy *Camcorder User*).

A combination of lighting and filters changes the mood to suit the scene.

This may sound difficult, and no-one would pretend it's something which can be sorted out quickly or easily. It takes time, and practice, and experience. But if you approach lighting like someone learning a new language, which in a sense it is, you should have few problems. Take your time, proceed step by step from what you CAN do to what you want to be ABLE to do, work within the limits of your equipment and your experience, and you may well be pleasantly surprised by the effects you are able to create. In fact, being able to build up scenes of progressively greater complexity through sensitive and careful lighting is one of the most vital parts of the challenge of professional production.

In time, when you feel happy enough with the rules of good lighting, you can begin to experiment with breaking those rules, in the interests of creating particular effects for individual reasons. For example, the rule of not shooting a subject against the light is worth breaking if what you want is a dramatic silhouette – but avoid direct sunlight, or any source of light so powerful that it overwhelms your chosen subject. Better by far to choose a soft, diffused light source, spread evenly over the background, such as a frosted glass window, or a window which is toned down by spreading a sheet of tracing paper over it to reduce the amount of light coming in.

You can also experiment with other variations on this theme. After all, a black silhouette is dramatic, but limited. Perhaps you want a little light and shade, to strive for a deliberate chiaroscuro effect. In that case, you shoot against the light, but lift the front of your subject's face with a light, effectively acting as a filler against the light flooding in from behind your subject. The result can be a very effective cameo portrait, ideal for heightening a particularly dramatic moment in whatever story you're telling. It doesn't have to be a scripted drama, either – someone in the act of blowing out the candles on a birthday cake could be highlighted in this way, as for that particular moment they are very much the centre of attention.

Finally, a word or two of warning. Lighting does use up a lot of power, and it does dissipate a lot of that power in heat as well as illumination. So you always need to be careful about overloading domestic electrical circuits. Don't risk blowing fuses by running too many lights from one source, don't risk domestic light fittings overheating and even catching fire, and don't leave lights on longer than necessary, especially if you have a whole battery of lights illuminating a room. You also need to be especially careful when moving lights or camera. Switch the lights off, and place the lens cap over the camera, so that there's no likelihood of powerful beams entering the lens and causing internal damage to the camera.

You also need to watch out for unwanted reflections off mirrors, panes of glass or any bright objects in the room. One option is to move them out of the way – if they seem essential to the scene, then you can buy special sprays to dull the reflecting surfaces, so that they don't transmit light back into the camera lens as a distractingly bright spot in the middle of an otherwise subdued scene. Other options to kill unwanted reflections include covering the reflectives surfaces with sticky tape, if the critical region is small enough, or spraying wider areas with a water mist to produce instant condensation, so that bright objects still look bright, without the reflections being troublesome in the overall scheme of things.

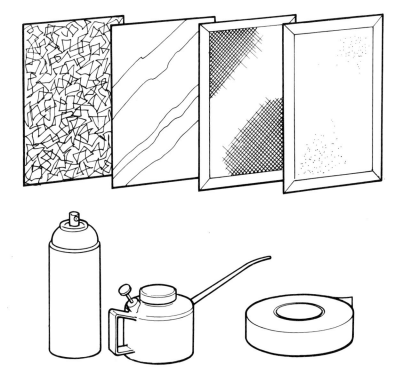

The effect of any video light can be enhanced by using a reflector or diffuser. From the left: crumpled kitchen foil; smooth kitchen foil: silk screen; tracing-paper screen.

Unwanted reflections can be eliminated by coating reflective surfaces with matt spray, water mist, or black tape.

Covering a procession by stationing yourself at a point on the route where the procession turns a corner or, as here, goes round a roundabout, to allow yourself a wider choice of shots.

Remember to position yourself so that after the initial approach shot (*above*) all traffic is apparently going through the frame in the same direction.

In this example, the direction is camera left to camera right.

LOCATION SHOOTING

Now it's time to go back into the bright outdoors, but this time with a rather more pragmatic approach. The practice shooting we have looked at so far has been of a planned, thought-out, almost scripted kind. In other words, we have approached the job of covering a subject with as much as possible under our own control. This is how a professional crew covering a scripted documentary, or a drama production, would work, moving from shot to shot in a controlled sequence, making the most of the time available to do the subject justice.

But many of the subjects we may wish to shoot would make that careful and considered approach impossible. They may move too quickly, or unpredictably, for the camera operator to capture a logical and attractive sequence as it happens. This means switching instead to a double approach – capturing reality as each opportunity arises, by quick reactions and a trained eye to spot each potential shot in time to capture it. But there will inevitably be gaps and omissions. Doing justice to one shot may mean you miss another almost equally attractive, or as essential to the sequence you're trying to build up. Capturing the whole of a movement, or an activity or a routine may take too long – so you need to known when to turn away and capture a cutaway, and when to turn back and return to the action you left, to take it a step further, and so on. There may be times when you need to re-create reality yourself by setting up the occasional shot as a piece of deliberate planning, but these will be rare. Instead of it being drama or documentary shooting, this tends to be closest to the kind of work done by the television news crews, struggling to capture the essential story behind each assignment as quickly, as safely, and as effectively as possible.

On the other hand, if your camera/home recorder combinaton allows you to edit the shots in a different order to make the finished programme, you do have a little extra flexibility you can make use of. You can shoot some cutaways before the event begins, or after it's over, and if you are careful about the subjects, then you needn't give the game away. Pick close-ups and small details which relate to the location you are in, but which won't look any different, whether the event is actually in progress or not – then you can edit them into the finished programme to bridge any gaps or cuts in the genuine action. But you will need to be careful that the sound-track matches properly, something which can be looked at during the dubbing stage. We will deal with this in a later chapter.

However, professional news crews have one great advantage: they can shoot their material in almost any order they like, that makes good sense. They know full well that the material can be edited afterwards to produce a logical and informative sequence. But even the most sophisticated video cameras allow for only strictly limited editing, which means it's wise to shoot everything in the order in which you want your audience to view it. We'll look at the options of insert editing later in the chapter. For the time being, let's limit ourselves to assemble editing, or shooting in strictly chronological order.

The first decision is to find a suitable subject – a real happening, which is not under your control in the same way as a family occasion like a picnic or an outing might be. You might pick a race meeting, or a sporting event like a regatta or a five-a-side football match, or a cycle race or a car rally, or a parade or a carnival. Let's begin by looking at a local carnival, with a procession containing everything from a beauty queen to a brass band, vintage buses and steam traction engines. With plenty of colour and plenty of movement, it's a subject which offers plenty of potential for the video camera, but a real challenge to the person who's operating it.

So begin by doing what the professionals do – 'recce' your location first. Go down to the route which the procession will follow, and look for interesting viewpoints. You might find the route crosses an attractive old bridge, which would set it in an interesting context. Or you may spot the chance for a shot from high above the procession, to produce a different perspective. Or it may be something a great deal simpler, like a right-angle bend along the processional route. At the very least, standing on the inside of the corner would give you two different angles on the procession as it approaches you up one street and recedes down the other, not to mention the slow sweep as it swings round the corner, right in front of your lens.

How do you choose your camera positions? This depends on all kinds of factors, like the length of the procession and the route it will follow. If it doubles back on its route, this gives you the priceless opportunity of two chances to shoot any section of it. If not, you may have to decide between following the tail end of the procession at one spot, and not having enough time to shoot the head of it at another promising location. So check whatever information is available on where the focal points of the procession are going to be. Does the carnival queen's carriage come at the front of the procession, or in the middle, or at the end? And does the procession itself tail off in squads of anonymous marchers, which don't produce such interesting pictures?

Another factor which may be worth thinking about is how easy, or difficult, it's likely to be moving from one place to another on the actual day. Will there be crowds in the way, will roads be closed, would you be allowed to cross the road ahead of the procession? Would you need to be in position before the crowds assemble, to guarantee an unobstructed view, in which case you might have to shoot the whole event from one spot, which calls for a great deal of ingenuity? All this pre-planning can make all the difference to the chances of success or failure on the day itself – and don't forget to check small but vital details like where the sun is going to be at the time of the procession. A viewpoint which seems perfect when you carry out the recce could be useless on the day because it would mean shooting straight into the sun.

Next, think about the equipment you may need. We'll assume that all the action will be taking place outdoors, in broad daylight, so that lighting isn't involved. The only real decision you need to take is whether or not you need a tripod. Carrying a tripod adds to the weight, and to the time you will need to move from place to place. On the other hand, having the chance of a steady mount for your camera gives you the option of long zooms or pans. These are worth bearing in mind, if your recce shows you a viewpoint where you can shoot a long telephoto shot of the whole procession approaching you up a hill, for example.

If you have someone to help you, who can carry the tripod when you don't need it, then the chances are you'll be glad of the extra opportunity for steady shots. On the other hand, there will be times when covering the subject well will mean the freedom and the speed which comes from using a hand-held camera. Picking the right method for the right shot, and knowing when to move the camera on and off the tripod, is one of the compelling reasons why this kind of practice shoot is essential.

When the day arrives, make sure you have all the spares and supplies you need, to do it justice. Will one tape be enough, or do you plan to use more? If so, have you the batteries to keep you running for the whole event, or will you have to husband battery power carefully if you're not going to run out at the vital moment of the procession's passing? Do you need to have any notes with you, to remind you of the order of events, or the order in which each section of the procession will pass your viewpoint?

Once your preparations have been made, it's time to take up your position, set up your camera and be ready for suitable shots. Don't wait for the procession to arrive before you start shooting – there may be some entertaining subjects there for the taking as people begin to arrive. Look out for school-children being marshalled by harassed teachers, eager spectators craning their necks down the road for the first sight of the procession, men setting up loud-speakers, police holding up traffic or putting up barriers to close off the roads while the procession passes. All these help to set the scene, and they help to add to the drama of when the procession actually arrives.

Be on the lookout, too, for potential cutaways. As we're setting out to shoot the event in the order of the completed programme, you can't actually shoot these cutaway shots now, to be edited into the right place after the day is over. But you CAN be on the lookout for suitable subjects – in the surrounding landscape – which will still be there when the procession arrives, so that when you want to bridge a jump-cut or allow a gap in the action, all you have to do is aim at your chosen cutaway subject and you have the shot you need, without having to search around you and miss the real action.

What kind of subjects fill these requirements will depend on the actual location – but anything connected with the event, like a line of coloured flags, flapping bravely in the breeze, or a poster advertising the event, or a colourful group of people on the far side of the street. You need as wide a choice as possible, since you don't know how many cutaways you might need, and you don't want to repeat them if you can help it. And you need subjects which are quite apart from the procession, so there are no problems of continuity involved. The shots, in short, have to be genuine cutaways, in that they represent a cut away from the main subject, the procession, but are still closely tied to the day, and to the action.

Once the procession comes into sight, you can exploit the fairly slow pace by cutting backwards and forwards between its approach, and other cutaways. Provided you alternate shots of the procession with cutaways, you don't need to keep shooting all the time – but if you can build up a rhythm whereby you shoot the procession's approach at regular intervals, it will produce a nice even pace in the finished programme. The right rhythm will depend on the speed with which the procession is approaching, but if your view is a long one down a straight road, then you could have as many as three or four shots between its first distant appearance and its arrival at your corner.

Once the head of the procession arrives at your corner, events will suddenly appear to speed up. Each section of the line-up which passes around the bend, on to the next stretch of the route, is lost to you – unless you can find another vantage point further along the route, which can be reached before the procession arrives there too. So pick your shots with care, and shoot only the best subjects. It's all too easy to concentrate on one moderate-quality shot, only to find when you remove your eye from the viewfinder that you've missed another potential shot which would have been much more worthwhile.

As always, be on the lookout for cutaways to widen and deepen the interest of the occasion.

The best cutaways are objects or people who are unlikely to move before the event is over!

This is one of the areas in which shooting a real-life event differs from a subject which is wholly, or partially under your control – as it would be in a scripted story you were shooting for your own purposes. Because every scene in a real-life event is unique and unrepeatable, you can't afford to immerse yourself completely in the shot you're shooting at any particular instant. You always have to be aware of other potential subjects all around you. And for some-one who can't rely on being able to edit the material afterwards, it imposes two extra requirements on you. One is to keep an eye open for the next potential shot, while you're shooting its predecessor – some camera operators do this literally, by using one eye to watch the viewfinder, but keeping the other eye open so that at least you have a measure of awareness of what is going on outside the narrow confines of your camera frame. And the second requirement is that you're able to end your present shot tidily, if you need to move quickly to another subject.

Let's assume that the procession, when it reaches you, is going to pass round the corner from left to right. You need at least one general shot to follow part of the procession through the corner, so that your audience will know where everything is. Then you can vary the action between medium shots, close-ups and cutaways, choosing the most interesting subjects you can find, as they pass. But remember that some shots may need more explanations than others – a close-up of the driving cab of a vintage lorry or double-decker bus is obvious enough, if your framing includes enough of the vehicle to tell the audience what it is. But a close-up of the complex valve-gear of a steam traction engine may be totally incomprehensible, unless you preceded it with a wider shot of the whole engine, or – if you didn't think of this in time – follow up with a shot of it disappearing round the corner, so your audience aren't left wondering about the subject, or the purpose, of your mystery shot.

With everything moving from right to left around you, you need to vary the camera angles as much as possible. You need to pick some subjects on their way into the corner, some on their way out, and some in the middle, for pace and variety. But unless a subject is really unusual, you can't afford to linger on it for too long, which means you have the problem of how to start and finish each shot. One option is to start off with a static frame, and have the subject move into it, and as the subject keeps on moving, you follow it with the camera. Remember, if you do, what we said earlier about 'walking room', or in this case 'moving room'. With a subject moving from left to right, you should try and frame it so that the main focus of interest is just to the left of the middle of your frame.

You can end your shot in one of two ways. A cut will look better if the camera is still at the moment when the shot ends. If the subject is still moving across your field of view quite quickly, which it will be doing at the mid-point of the corner, then all you do is bring your panning movement smoothly to a stop, and the subject will move on to clear the frame. At that point, you end your shot – and this gives you the option of ending the shot quickly whenever you want to move on to another subject. If you're following a subject right through to the exit from the corner, though, all you have to do is wait for it to be moving almost straight away from you, and you can end your shot with the subject still in frame, but with the camera static, making a neat cut to your next shot.

There's only one problem with this kind of cutting in and out of shots, and that is that the sudden arrival or departure of the subject means you have to start and finish with an empty frame. So the best way to do this is to find something in the static background to the scene which will still fill the frame before the subject arrives, and another one which will fill the frame once you allow the subject to leave it behind. Anything visually interesting will do – a quaint old shopfront, an advertising hoarding, a group of schoolchildren watching the procession. It will decide the length of some of your shots, but it does mean that you needn't have every pan starting and ending in an empty frame.

With these different options at your disposal, it should be possible to vary the material you shoot, through the whole course of the procession – but bear in mind you could also try the occasional elevated shot, if your recce showed you somewhere to stand which was high enough to look down on the procession – or if you can get permission to shoot from an upstairs window close to your chosen corner. And by lifting the magnifying lens clear of the viewfinder so that you can see it at a distance, you can lower the camera to the pavement to shoot a low-angle shot from there as another variation.

In fact, as you're going to need an ending shot to tell the audience they've seen the whole sequence, one possibility is to wait for the very end of the procession, and then lay the camera down on the edge of the roadway set for a long shot. If you have your adjustments right, the final shot will show the road surface filling most of the frame, narrowing to a distant perspective with the tail of the procession disappearing slowly into the background.

One final point, before the action finally finishes. If you are editing the shots in a different sequence to make the finished programme, it is always a good idea to make sure you have plenty of sound effects to use over all the cutaways you may have shot before the action started. So point your camera at anything you like, and record a few minutes of material purely for the sound effects you are picking up – the cheers of the crowd, the noise of a band, or whatever. It'll be worth its weight in gold later.

Covering this kind of event from one particular location has one advantage. Everything in your range of vision – everything involved with the procession that is – will be moving either directly towards you, or directly away from you, or crossing from left to right in front of you. So there will be no temptation, and probably no opportunity, to commit the sin of 'crossing the line' – moving across to the other side of the route so that some shots of the procession would show people and vehicles moving from right to left. The problem with this kind of change is that it's difficult for the audience to realise that you're seeing the same movement along the same route from a viewpoint on the other side. Seeing a shot with people moving from left to right cutting straight to people moving from right to left can create confusion in the minds of the audience, because it LOOKS as if everyone has changed their minds and are now going back the way they came.

The kinds of ideas, advice and techniques we've been talking about here can be used for all kinds of events where you want to record what's actually happening. There are times when, for very good reasons, you will actually want to cross the line. The best way to do this is to make sure that the shot before the first one from the new viewpoint is one where the main action is coming straight towards you, or straight away from you. Then the change in the direction of movement won't appear so confusing – and provided you bear the same requirements in mind, you're free to cross the line as many times as you like. It's all part of the very necessary duty to keep your audience in mind the whole time – something we'll now explore in shooting a short sequence where, just for a change, everything IS under your control.

Don't 'cram' the viewer – wide open scenes can be effective.

THE GRAMMAR OF PROGRAMME-MAKING

Chapter 6

Now we're ready to shoot a subject in the same way as professional drama or documentary producers do: shot by shot according to a prepared script. At this stage we shall confine ourselves to the simplest of subjects, but it's vital to remember one requirement which is equally important, whatever level of expertise you're bringing to bear on the subject. Because these will be essentially YOUR shots, and not your capturing of images which are there already, as was the case in the last chapter, you will need to work specially hard to make them interesting, involving and varied. With all the action under your control, you have no-one else to blame if shots are boring, badly composed, or confusing in any way.

We need to pick a subject with plenty of movement, but a simple theme – a combination which allows maximum creativity. This time, we'll use for our example a short trip in a new car. The action will begin with our proud car owner leaving the house to take his brand-new car out for a spin – no complicated dramatic or comedy effects, just the simplest possible story told through the pictures and the sequences you choose. How do you start?

The first step is to make a shot list. This is easier than keeping track of everything through memory, or having to think after each shot is completed, of what you can shoot to follow it up. It means concentrating on a mental image of a television screen, and decid-ing which sequence of images you're going to put down on your shooting list to tell the story you want to tell. So let's begin at the most logical place – at the beginning of your story.

What should your first, establishing shot be? One option might be to show the car, and the front door of the house, in the same shot, to create an impression in the audience's mind that someone is about to appear through the door, and come out to the car. But let's think a little more deeply – is there any way of establishing the car as a new one, the owner's pride and joy? One option might be to zoom out of (or zoom in on) the 'year letter' on the number plate of the car, which at least shows it's an up-to-date model. But a better way might be to emphasise the freshness and cleanliness of this brand-new vehicle by looking for a reflection of the house in the chrome or the windows of the car, and then cutting, or panning to the front door of the house, to link those two parts of the subject closely in the minds of the audience.

What should the next shot show? You can either prolong the expectation that, sooner or later, someone is going to come out and drive off, by shooting some more cutaways of the car. This is worth doing if you can find anything else which shows newness, freshness, pride of ownership. Polished paintwork, protective covers on the seats, even a very low reading on the dashboard mileometer might be worth considering. If you have enough time and energy, and you want to build up the sequence more ambitiously, you could actually consider cutting backwards and forwards between the silent, empty, waiting car in the road outside the house, and the owner inside the house getting ready for the drive. In other words, a shot of the car would be followed by a shot of the owner putting his coat on, a shot of the empty seats by a shot of the car keys on a hall table, and a hand picking them up, a shot from the driving seat of the car over the top of the steering wheel to the front door of the house, perhaps as it opens for the owner to step out and walk out to the car.

All these are genuine options, some needing more trouble and preplanning than others. You may need to move the car to the right spot, relative to the house, to frame the steering wheel/front door shot, and you would certainly need some kind of cue to tell the driver when to open the door and walk out to the car. If you shout, it's going to be picked up on the sound-track (see Chapter 10), so one option is to agree a pre-arranged delay so that you both know when the action is going to begin. Where timing is especially critical, you can sometimes arrange for a helper who is out of shot to wave a cue to the person you're waiting to shoot.

Either way, you may find that the first time you record a shot – the first 'take' in professional parlance – isn't precisely as you want it. If that's the case, you need to repeat it, several times if necessary, until the timing and everything else is exactly as you want it. And as you're editing the sequence within the camera, you'll need to wind the tape back to the beginning of the shot for each new take to be recorded over its predecessor. Although it involves a lot of extra trouble, it does mean that when the shot DOES work properly, that's the only version you're left with on the tape, so that you can move on to the next shot.

Before we leave the opening of the door and the walk to the car, let's look at another completely different way of doing it. The first suggestion was virtually a treatment of the action from the car's point of view – but it's equally possible to start the story from the owner's point of view instead. All you need to do is start with the action inside the house: the putting on of the coat, the picking up of the car keys, the walk to the door. You can even intercut shots of the owner putting on his coat and picking up the keys with a shot of the car waiting out in the road, shot through the window of the room the owner is in. You can experiment with putting the camera close up to the glass, so that it looks as if the shot is recorded from an outside viewpoint, without the time and trouble of actually going outside – but you must remember to readjust the white balance to an 'outdoors' setting. Or you could shoot the car from further back inside the room, to suggest you're looking at it through the owner's eyes – but if so, you need to bear two more points in mind.

We saw earlier how video cameras are unhappy with very sharp contrasts – like the contrast between the light level inside a room and that seen outside, through the window. But where the focus of interest is what you actually see through that window, then you can make sure the camera's iris is set for the light level outside. All you will see of the inside of the room is the edge of the window-frame, and possibly the curtains, in silhouette, which could provide you with a neat way of suggesting the owner's eye-view of his car. But you could make the point crystal-clear by shooting the owner's face, looking out through the window, either before or after the shot of the car framed in the window opening. And any other shots which you can think of to emphasise the owner's intentions, to go for a drive, are worth bearing in mind before shooting his move out of the house – a look at his watch, or even a glance at a road map, might help to emphasise the point without making it too laboured and obvious to the audience.

So our owner decides it's time to go, and makes for the door. You need to split up all these actions into different shots and different angles. You might try to shoot the walk to the front door from halfway up the stairs, to give you a different perspective on his actions. You will have shot the keys in a big close-up, his face looking out of the window in a medium close-up, so that this one is something of a long-shot – at least, it's as much of a long-shot as is going to be possible within the confines of the house. Now you have the problem of shifting from the inside of the house to the outside. What's the most effective way of making that transition?

There are several different ways of doing this. One is to stay within the house, as the driver walks out through the door – but don't wait for him to close the door behind him, as that's going to cut you off from the action. Let him close the door and walk away, but stop the shot with the door wide open. Then you can move outside, readjust and rebalance the camera, and set yourself up for a shot of the door opening, and the driver emerging. Now you have to decide the best point at which to cut to the new shot, and how far to follow him out to the car. If he has to go through a garden gate, this might offer a natural punctuation point to cut out of the shot, so all you have to decide now is where to cut from the previous shot.

You can make a neat cut by switching from the indoors shot to the outdoors one when the door is wide open. Your viewpoints are different, the angles are different, especially if you have chosen a viewpoint to allow you to pan and follow the driver all the way to the gate. If you were shooting this sequence for a professional production, you would be able to shoot a walk to the car from a series of different viewpoints, and then decide at the editing stage exactly where to cut between one version and another. Without the advantage of an expensive editing suite, you will have to take that decision while you're shooting, and that means some delicate timing to make for a smooth, well-edited sequence. Let's take one edit in particular: the cut from the opening of the door inside the house, to the opening of the door from outside, followed by the driver stepping out, closing the door behind him, and walking to the car.

First of all, you need to find the point on the shot you have just recorded at which you want to cut to the new shot. To make things as smooth and as simple as possible, it should be a natural pause in the movement – let's say the moment when, having stepped through the front door, the driver half-turns to close it, before continuing his walk to the car. You now need to start the new shot at that point in the tape, but that's not all – you have to make sure your new shot starts with the driver continuing the movement from the point where you choose to cut out of the previous shot. And it's all a matter of very careful timing.

As we saw in the opening chapter, most of today's home video cameras are able to work on the 'assemble edit' mode. This means, broadly, that the camera can be set up with the tape set at the point where you want to make the edit, and the controls set at 'pause', so that all you need to do is press the 'start' button and the new shot will begin recording immediately. This means that your action must be instantaneous if there is not to be a perceptible hesitation at the moment of the edit, which is going to make the cut look laboured and contrived.

The best way to avoid this is to ask your 'driver' to repeat the action he did before, from the very beginning. Then you can watch for the right moment to press the 'start' button to begin the new shot. This is far easier than trying to put him in the start position for the new shot, and making sure you allow the right interval for him to react to your shouted cue, and to begin his movement from the cut point. But make sure he repeats the action as precisely as he can. If he turns a different way, or if he uses a different hand to close the door, or turns his head a different way, it may show up on the edit and spoil the smoothness of the transition from one shot to the next.

This shot follows him out to the garden gate, where you can set up another edit. Follow him out through the gate from your present position, then set up for the next shot. Try and think of a completely different viewpoint this time – perhaps a low-angle shot with the camera resting on the pavement at the rear end of the car looking upwards to him opening the door and climbing in. By framing the shot tightly beside the car, you don't need to see the garden gate, which means your edit doesn't need to be timed quite as precisely this time.

It's still important, though, that the time taken for the driver to step from the gate into the frame of your shot is about right, so you may as well ask him to do the walk down the path again. Find the point where you intend to cut out of the previous shot and set the tape at that point, with the camera in the 'pause' mode. Set up the framing and the focus, and if necessary, ask your driver to do a 'walk through' – walk through the shot as he will do when you're record-ing, so that you can concentrate on how it looks in the viewfinder.

Then all you have to do is ask him to go back to the beginning of his walk – often called the 'first position' to distinguish it from any other special instructions or places on the way through the shot. When you're completely ready, tell him to start his walk by calling 'action', and when you see him closing the gate behind him, press the 'start' button, and the timing of the shot, and his walk into frame, and the climb into the car, should be perfect. Once again, if you are editing the programme by copying it on to your VCR, rather than simply building it up shot by shot on the cassette in the camera, then you will find these shots a lot easier to cope with. Simply make sure you start the recording before the action, and that you don't stop before the action is finished. Then you can find the precise points to cut from the indoor shot to the outdoor shot when you edit the master copy together — provided you make each shot longer than it needs to be, you will always have enough material.

We now need to see the car started and driven away, a procedure which takes a surprisingly long time in reality. One of the powers of capturing this action on tape is that we can compress this time by choosing our shots carefully. Rather than watch him settling into the seat, fastening the seat belt, putting the keys into the ignition, starting the engine, engaging first gear, checking the road for traffic and then driving off, we can suggest all these things by a simple sequence of shots.

We have just seen the driver climb into the car. We can now move to the front of the car to shoot through the windscreen – watch out for reflections – as he fastens the safety belt. Then we can shoot the exhaust pipe as he starts the engine – the vibration and the puff of exhaust smoke say exactly what's happening, without any continuity problems. We can see the driver checking the mirror, or turning round to look behind him, by setting the camera so that we can see the driver's face through the wing-mirror. And finally, when the car moves off, you can pick a close-up subject like the tyres, or the indicator light (if he uses the indicators to warn other traffic that he's about to pull away from the kerb), and simply leaving the camera in a stationary position as the car pulls away – so that a shot which begins as a big-close-up becomes translated into a wide shot by virtue of the car's pulling away and leaving a clear view of the road and the surroundings. But it's worth trying this one out first, in case you have to adjust the focus as the car moves away.

Having got the car moving, we have several options in capturing the journey on tape. One is to select a series of viewpoints along the route to see the car passing the camera. But choose a variety of places where the shots will be varied enough to make it worthwhile to move from one to another and set up the camera afresh each time. One might be a long shot of a straight approach up a hill towards the camera, where you can pick up the car in the distance on the end of a zoom, and zoom back slowly as the car comes closer to capture the approach in full until the car fills the screen and passes out of frame as it passes the camera. You'll need a tripod to do justice to that one – and you can't make every passing shot last as long, or it will slow down the pace of the sequence too much.

Vary it by shooting another version of the car passing through a set of curves where the action will involve a pan backwards and forwards instead of a long straight approach. Sometimes you can ask your driver to make two passes by the same camera position. Shoot the first one as an approach shot, stopping when the car passes out of frame as it passes your camera. Then turn the camera around (but staying on the same side of the road) and point it in the right direction to capture the car receding in the distance AFTER it's passed the camera position. Set up, as before, with the tape at the right point for the end of the previous shot, and ask the driver to go back down the road and pass you once again. As you sense the car is about to pass you, press the 'start' button and begin the new shot, following the car through until it disappears round the next corner.

If you're lucky, the edit will work perfectly and give you a smooth transition between the two shots. If there's a slight mistiming, it might be worth setting up the second shot again, and repeating it until you get it right. It's valuable experience, which you can use for anything from a car chase to covering a motor race by shooting approach and receding shots of the same car on successive laps.

Passing shots are just one of the three ways to capture the journey our driver is making. The other two methods will bring you much more material, as you can keep recording for longer, for a given camera position. First, you can set up inside the car, by sitting in the front passenger seat, and turning your camera to look at the driver's face as he controls the car, watches the traffic and even admires the view. Or you can sit in the back and look over his shoulder, so that you can frame a shot which includes the back of his head, his left arm and shoulder and his view of the road ahead – better, in this case, to ensure the iris is set for the view of the road outside, and to accept the driver as a mere silhouette in this framing. An alternative is to reset the iris for the light level inside the car, and using the back of the front passenger seat to steady your camera, to shoot close-up cutaways of the speedometer, the driver changing gear, and so on.

Finally, you can shoot the exterior of the car by moving with it. All you need is another car, which can travel in front of the car you're shooting, or even behind it from time to time; and some kind of facility which allows you to shoot ahead or behind. It might be a soft-top, it might have a sunshine roof, or it might be an estate car with a lifting tailgate or a window which can be wound down to give you a clear view of the road behind. The main priorities are to try to hold your camera as steadily as possible against the bumps and shocks a car experiences even over smooth roads, and it's also a good idea to brief the driver you're filming to try and stay at approximately the same distance ahead or behind you, to minimise the need to refocus.

When you have a little more experience, you can try waving the driver up to you for more close-up shots, or instructing him to drop back for wider shots, or even, when it's safe, you can wave him to overtake, to give a way of ending the shot other than a simple cut to something else. Between these three types of shot, you can cover the entire journey, making as much use as you can of the different kinds of background – town, country, and suburban – he's likely to be passing en route. But the biggest problem you face is the lack of flexibility with editing.

Unlike a professional crew, who could shoot all the in-car material in one session, and all the tracking shots (shooting from another car) at another single session, then all the passing shots in turn, creating the final sequence at the editing stage – you may well have to shoot everything in the order you want to see it appearing on the tape. It will take longer this way, and you'll need to take a great deal more trouble, but in the end it's all perfectly possible. It CAN be done, and the result of a carefully built-up sequence can be ample compensation for all the time and effort involved.

Some cameras do have an extra facility which could be useful here – an 'insert edit' capability. What this means in practice is that you can go back and record a new shot over an existing shot, with a clean edit at either end. This is called an 'overlay shot' in television editing, and it's a useful, if limited capability for a sequence like this.

Essentially, it means you have to record a shot which is long enough to make an overlay shot in the middle worth while. Then you identify the points in that shot where you want the overlay shot to start and finish. You mark the finishing point on the tape, by moving to that point and then setting the reset button and pressing the memory button. Then you wind back the tape to the point where you want the overlay shot to start, and you put the camera into 'pause' at that point. When you have the shot set up, you press the 'start' button, just as you would with an assemble edit. The camera will start recording the new, overlay, shot with a smooth edit from the previous shot – but when the tape reaches the preset point for the end of the shot, it will cut automatically back to the previous shot.

The drawback is that you can only decide the length of your overlay shot before you shoot it, not while you're shooting it – though the tape counter will give you some warning of the end of the shot, as it counts down towards the '0000' indication of the preset end edit point. This means that you need to choose your cutaway subjects carefully, so that exact timings are not too important. For example, if you shot a long tracking sequence, then you could insert one or more overlay shots of the driver inside the car, cutting them to fit whatever space you set for them. But inserting a passing shot, though it would make a great deal of sense to be able to add these one after another at various points in the tape, would be more difficult, as they tend to have a definite beginning, where the car comes into view, and an equally definite ending, where the car vanishes out of frame at the end.

There are two possible ways around this problem. One is to go to the extra trouble of following the car through the shot in the camera viewfinder as a rehearsal, timing the length of the shot exactly. Then you can send your driver back to the start, and shoot the whole passing movement in the hope that the timings will still be the same.

Another way of solving the problem is to insert two shots in direct succession – an approach shot, and a receding shot – but with one slight variation. Insert the approach shot exactly as before, but this time deliberately prolong it until the car is well past the camera. Then set up your receding shot, making the edit start at the point where the previous shot showed the car passing the camera, and setting the end point where you expect the car to be some distance away. Provided the opening edit (which IS under your control) is accurate, the sequence will work, because an edit from a receding shot of a car down a straight road can be made anywhere you like in a tracking shot or a shot inside the car – provided there's nothing sufficiently obvious about the background scenery to reveal that the two shots are recorded at completely different places.

On the other hand, if you can edit from your camera to your home VCR, you are left much freer to experiment with cuts like these – you will be surprised how quickly your instinctive sense of timing tells you *exactly* when to cut from one shot to the next.

Basically the system works like this: after you have finished shooting, connect the camera up to your VCR according to the instructions in the handbook. You load the tape on which you want to build up the finished programme into the VCR, and set the machine to 'record' and then to the 'pause' mode. You then look for the first shot you want to put into the finished programme by loading the relevant tape into the camera. Play it back through the viewfinder, until you reach the point where you want the shot to start – then set the camera to 'pause'. Then, following the instructions for your particular camera/VCR combination, you can start editing the programme by copying the shot from the tape in the camera on to the tape in the VCR. When you want the shot to end, you can pause the tapes again, find the next shot you want to edit (which can be earlier or later on the same camera tape, or even on a different camera tape altogether) and then repeat the process. It is an option which offers complete freedom in putting a programme together.

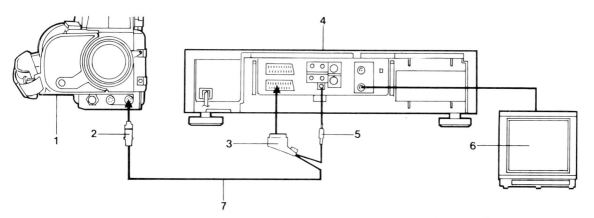

An example of how your camera be connected directly to your home VCR for flexible editing.
(1) Camera/playback unit
(2) To AV out (3) To AV input
(4) Recording deck
(5) To 'pause' connector
(6) TV (7) AV output cable.

There's one more way of punctuating a sequence like this, particularly when you want to suggest that more time has passed than can be implied even with careful editing. One way that professional producers do it is by mixing or dissolving slowly between one shot and the next – but this means specialist, and expensive editing equipment. You can, however, create a similar effect by fading to black at the end of the shot before the jump in time, then fading from black up to the next shot in the sequence, which could be in a different locality, and show a completely different subject. What would be confusing in a normal edit can work well with this softer transition between the shots.

Controlling a fade to black, and the succeeding fade FROM black is simple enough – see Chapter 1 – but when would you use this effect? That depends on a number of different factors, and it can only depend in the end on what kind of effect you're trying to create. In this case, though, once you'd thoroughly established the idea of the journey, you could fade between a tracking shot of the car travelling through a country setting, which we have implied is not too far away from the house where it all started, to a busy town centre. You could even make a succession of fades to bridge a whole series of different backgrounds, depending on the time and distance you have available and the number of contrasts you can find. If you're able to fade between a hilly stretch of road, a section through a forest, a stretch crossing a river or beside the sea, and a section through an industrial landscape, you can imply the journey has taken in half of Britain!

Finally, let's try to think how to end the story. Simply shooting the driver pulling up outside the house and disappearing back through the front door might be just a little too tame, even for a practice shoot like this. Try to think of some kind of punchline to the story which can be told in pictures, without it being too complicated.

For example, you could arrange your sequence inside the car to show the driver suddenly being unsure of which direction he could take. One of your roadside shots could show the car approaching a fork in the road, and swinging backwards and forwards between the two alternatives, before settling for one at the last minute. Or you could shoot the car passing a road junction and signposts. The car stops, the driver climbs out and walks back to look at the signpost, scratching his head. Then, from another angle, you can shoot him rummaging in the glovebox to produce a road atlas, where he looks through page after page, without finding what he wants. Try to think of other ways of developing this idea until, as your last frame, you can show him slumped in the seat with the map thrown out of the window and holding his head in his hands in despair.

Another ending might be more conventional – but with a surprise at the last moment. The driver finally arrives back outside the house, from which he started. He climbs out of the car, looks fondly at it after closing the door and locking it. He tosses the keys in the air, tries to catch them, and misses. You show a close-up of his face looking down, so that he can pick them up, and his expression changing from pleasure to horror. Then the last shot is one looking down, from his own viewpoint, to a grid just in front of his feet, down which we assume the keys have just disappeared.

Whichever way you choose to round off the sequence, it should have contained some valuable lessons, and some worthwhile experience. Try to follow it with several more visual stories, developing towards more expert and more ambitious treatments of other simple themes. Apart from improving your expertise with the camera, it will help you to think automatically in terms of the grammar of showing a story in pictures – an essential basis for more complex subjects.

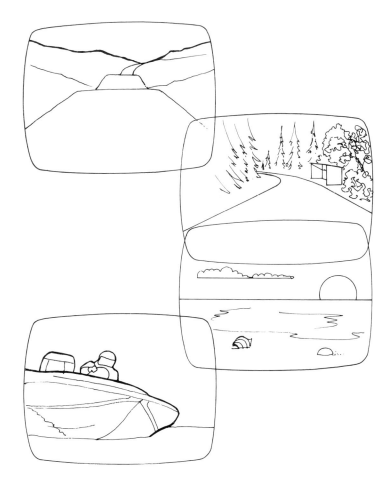

Fading between contrasting scenes can indicate that a journey has taken in half of the country!

SOUND

So far, we've been concentrating throughout on the pictures, apart from the need to record words of our contributors and presenters in the previous chapter. But that's one of the supreme advantages of video over film. It carries its own sound track, automatically kept in synchronisation with the picture in a way which ciné-film makers can only envy. As they have to record their sound on a separate audio tape, they have to take precautions which will allow them to match sound to pictures later on. Normally they start each shot with a clapper board which is held up in front of the camera and snapped shut very positively. The number of the shot is shown on the board, and the clapper-board operator calls out that number so the reference and the noise of the clapper-board closing, is picked up on the audio tape. Then the film and the sound tape can be lined up in the editing machine so that sounds and pictures match precisely.

None of that is needed with a video camera. In fact, since all home video cameras are equipped with directional microphones mounted on top of the camera body, it's quite difficult NOT to record sound when you're shooting pictures. You don't even have to think about it – up to a point. But the fact still remains that for the quality of the sound to match a well-constructed picture sequence, then it's worth paying some extra thought to this often-neglected branch of video programme-making.

Let's begin by looking at microphones. The kind of microphone you'll find supplied as part of your camera kit is probably a compromise between the highly directional microphones like rifle mikes and the omni-directional mikes often used for specific effects. These terms refer, not to the way a microphone works, nor even to its quality, but to the area from which it picks up its sound. High-quality rifle mikes can be made to pick up sound over a very narrow arc indeed – as the name implies, you almost have to aim them, like a rifle, at the subject whose sound you want to record. This can be useful where you want to concentrate on a particular sound, cutting out as much as possible of any other background sounds which might detract from your objective.

The omni-directional mike comes in when you have exactly the opposite objective. You want the complete sound picture from all points of the compass, without sounds from any one direction being particularly over-emphasised at the expense of the others. Where you need all-round atmosphere, rather than the sounds made by a particular subject, then this is the mike you need.

What you get, fastened to your video camera, is usually a combination of the two. It will pick up sounds most clearly from the direction in which you're pointing the camera, but it will also pick up some of the background sounds from other directions too. This can be fine, when that kind of mixture of sound inputs is what you want – but you can achieve much more if the balance between

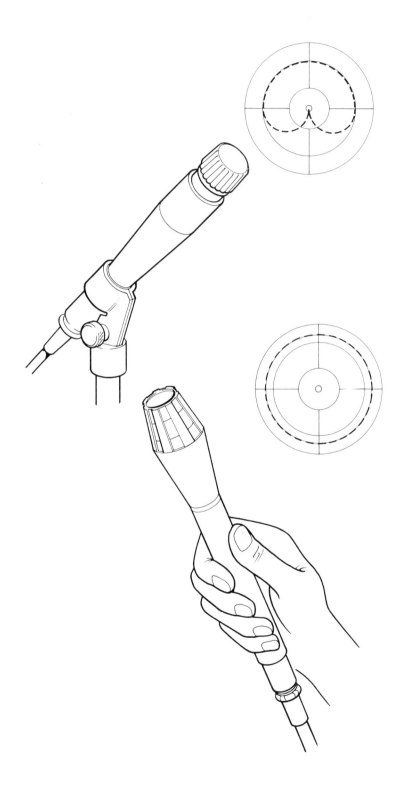

A unidirectional mike is more sensitive to sound from one direction in particular. Rifle mikes can be used to focus in on a particular sound source (like someone speaking against a noisy background). The more common cardioid mike shown here does pick up some background noise as well – hence the heart-shaped response curve which accounts for its name.

Omnidirectional mikes pick up sound with more or less equal sensitivity from all directions. Their main use is to pick up general atmosphere to mix with the sound of a particular subject.

subject sound and background sound were more under your own control.

Fortunately, microphones – even quite good-quality microphones – are a great deal cheaper than video cameras. This means you should invest in two, if you possibly can: a directional mike and an omni-directional mike, to give you the kind of selectivity your camera mike won't provide. Check that the connections will fit your cam-corder combination – in most cases connecting another mike to the system automatically switches off the camera mike, so that your sound will still come from a single source.

There's another advantage to using separate microphones. In addition to being able to choose the sounds your camera will pick up, you can also connect them to the camera with extra-long leads, giving you another measure of selectivity. Instead of having to record all sounds from the camera position, you can move the microphone to the source of the sound you particularly want. This has two advantages. You can pick out individual sounds, which allow you to make more of them, to create a dramatic effect. For example, if our going-for-a-drive sequence had some kind of sinister motive, then the total absence of background sound, coupled with the clicking of the doorlatch, the crunch of footsteps on the path, and the creak of the gate, all recorded through a mike much closer to the action than the camera, could have heightened the drama.

The other advantage is in recording an interview, or a prepared piece being delivered to camera. The closer your microphone is to your subject, the less it will be inclined to pick up other sounds. It can be quite surprising how noisy the world is, even in apparently tranquil locations: traffic noise, aircraft high overhead, even bird-song, can be picked up all too well at times. This can partially blanket the words and, if it's a sound which isn't present all the time, can give the game away when you have to edit a contributor's response to a question. In the first part of his answer, you may hear a car or an aeroplane in the background – then suddenly it disappears, revealing that the tape has been edited at that point.

One more point which you must bear in mind when using microphones. It's quite acceptable for someone to hold a microphone when they're delivering a piece to camera, or when they're interviewing someone. But as a general rule, if you can conceal the microphone, it's better to do so. For interviews, you can buy small lapel mikes which appear rather like a small brooch or tiepin, especially if you conceal the cord under shirt or jacket. Or you can hold the mike on the end of a boom (fastening the mike to the end of a broom handle with a bandage of adhesive tape is an easy expedient) and use this to aim the microphone at the subject, from just out of shot. Whatever you do, don't let the mike or the mike cable appear in shot, unless it's being used by the presenter. That's on a par with getting the camera crew, or the director or even the instruction manual into the shot, or having a contributor look at the camera and ask 'Do you want me to say my bit now?'. We all know these things happen, but keeping them out of the programme means taking that little extra trouble to produce professional re-sults. So even if you need to place your mike on the far side of the scene to pick up the sound you want, camouflage it, and the cable, as thoroughly as you can.

There is still, however, one serious limitation in the sound you can apply to your video programmes. On a professional production, the sound-track you hear is a mixture of people speaking to camera, interviews, background sound, and special effects added to heighten a particular mood, together with music as well – in other words, a mixture of several different tracks at a time. But since you're only recording on one sound channel, your options are more limited. If you record the presenter, or an interview, then you can't add any other effects at that point. If you want to add a voice-over commentary, then you will blot out the existing sound by recording over it. Going back to the steam-train example, if you were to speak into the microphone afterwards, using the audio dub facility on the recorder to add a commentary explaining the background to the scene, you'd lose all the sounds which were part of the atmosphere on the day: the hissing of the steam, the voice of the station loudspeaker, the chatter of children, the whistle of the guard, and the noise of departure. So what can you do about it?

There are in fact two remedies. One of them is to decide what you're going to say before the shoot, and then speak into the microphone when it will pick up your voice along with all the background sounds. But apart from giving you yet another thing to worry about on the location, this is a difficult and rather inflexible method. You may change your mind over what you want to say, you may trip over your words and need to start again – in each case you'd have to record the whole shot again, and the train might pull out by the time you finally managed to get your act together.

Better to add your commentary afterwards, as part of a properly mixed sound track, as the professionals do. By timing your com-mentary to the finished programme, you can say exactly what you want to say (see Chapter 10 on scripting a commentary), and you can suit the words to the pictures and to the timing of the programme, for the most professional result. But how can you do that without obliterating the existing sound-track? The answer is, you take a leaf from the professionals' book, by taking the sound track from the camera tape and mixing it separately before copying it back on to the finished programme. And for that, you'll need some extra equipment.

The first essential is a pair of audio recorders – either reel-to-reel or audio cassette recorders will do the job equally well. The first step is to copy the sound track from the edited programme, from start to finish on to one of the recorders. Having written your script, and timed each of the sections to make sure your words will fit between the parts where you need to hear the sounds, or the words of other people already on the tape, then you need to record this commentary on to the second recorder, with the first recorder playing in the background. For a really professional result, you need to turn the playback level of the first recorder up and down to fit the parts of the programme where you're adding the commentary. The background sounds should be clear where you're not speaking, and subdued (though still there) when you're delivering the commentary.

Given quiet surroundings and a reasonably good quality pair of recorders, you can copy and recopy sound without the loss of quality you would get with recopying videotapes to the same extent. In fact, you could recopy the sound track on to the first recorder, to add background music from a record or another tape, and you can also add extra sound effects from any of the collection of discs made available by the BBC and other organisations, purely for the amateur film and programme-maker.

The final step is one you only take when you have your sound track mixed to your own satisfaction, with the voices clear, the sound effects discernible without being overwhelming and the music sufficient to heighten the mood of the programme whenever it appears. You now need to copy this mixed tape back on to the video cassette, using the audio-dub facility. But you're now in the same position as the cine-film maker – with sound and pictures on separate tapes, you need a reference mark to make sure they're properly synchronised.

In this case, the easiest way to do it is to play the audio tape and the videotape side by side, to make sure that the sound effects recorded on the day also run side by side. This is easy enough to do, since the sound-track will only be erased from the video cassette when you dub this mixed tape on to it. Once you've got both sources properly lined up (and take several attempts at playing them back together to make sure your synchronisation is as perfect as you can make it) and you're ready to go. Check your recording levels during a dry run, then press the audio dub control, set both re-corders running, and away you go. Your reward should be a prop-erly mixed and balanced sound-track, synchronised to the pictures you've edited into the programme, and with voices, sound effects and music blended together to produce a highly professional result – well worth the extra trouble taken to produce it.

GRAPHICS

Virtually every television programme you'll ever see uses graphics somewhere, if only for the opening and closing titles, to give you the name of the programme and the names of the people who helped to make it. But graphics appear in all kinds of other roles too – to identify people being interviewed, to reinforce facts and figures being quoted in the programme, to introduce different parts of the programme, to identify locations and to provide additional background information of every type. But where professional programme makers can produce lettering quickly, using keyboard-type graphics generators which allow you to type in the lettering you want to see on the screen, and then to decide on its size and positioning, until recently home video producers have had nothing in the way of similar facilities to rely on.

But the latest generation of video cameras now frequently feature character generators as part of the package, or as an optional extra which can be bought separately. They look like a television remote-control, with a series of buttons to control different functions and to provide a complete alphanumeric (letters and figures) keyboard, and they are normally plugged into the socket used by the electronic viewfinder on the camera body. While they're in use, you plug the viewfinder lead into another connection on the character generator, so you can still see the characters you're selecting.

The object is to be able to write any captions which you want to superimpose on whatever it is you're shooting – a very useful facility for naming individuals or locations, or creating opening and closing titles. Different buttons allow you to select capitals or lower-case letters, or to control the captions you write to occupy different parts of the screen. You can produce a whole series of captions, as cards, and you can control when one is replaced by the next, the time clearly depending on how much information you've written on the screen in each case. Generally speaking, you need to allow the audience time to read each screenload of information twice, fairly slowly, before switching to the next. And you can produce a long list of titles, which you can set to continue scrolling up the screen over whatever the camera is shooting at the time – an ideal way to produce professional end-credit shots to close your programme with a list of those who helped or contributed in any way.

But the usefulness of this extra facility doesn't stop there. If you wanted to put over a particular piece of information as a graph, with a written title and a set of pictures, then because the character generator combines the letters you set with the picture seen by the camera, you can create the graph in reality, and add the title and the figures electronically. All you need to do is find a sheet of coloured paper, add a pair of axes and the line of the graph with coloured tape in a contrasting colour, and the character generator can be used to do the rest.

Set the graph up on a backing card to hold it flat and mount the camera on the tripod. Point the camera squarely at the card – unless the axis of the lens is perpendicular to the paper, the horizontals and verticals on the paper (like the axes on the graph) won't look straight – and frame the graph carefully, leaving space for the characters you want to add. Try adding the titles and the figures you want to incorporate into the graph, moving them where necessary, and reframing the picture where there isn't enough space for the letters you want to fit in. Since this is a static shot, all the work is in the preparation. Once the diagram is finished to your satisfaction, you can then record it for as long as it should take the audience to absorb the information which it contains.

If you don't have this kind of facility on your camera, then that doesn't limit you to having to do without graphics altogether. Granted, you won't be able to superimpose lettering on pictures in quite the same way, but a little ingenuity can still enable you to produce some varied and sophisticated effects. All you need is a set of cards of the right size and colour, and you can either draw in your own lettering and symbols, or use sheets of dry print letters like Letraset, which you simply rub off the backing paper and on to your card exactly where they're needed.

Let's begin with the cards first. These need to be cut to the proportions of the television screen – three units deep and four across – and an ideal size would be about a foot across by about nine inches deep. Much smaller than that, and your lettering would have to be cramped – much larger and most of the standard sizes of Letraset would be too small to be read easily when played back on the screen. It's a good idea if the cards themselves are pale buff or grey, since these will appear almost white on the screen, but would be less likely to produce troublesome reflections than a pure white card might do. And an additional tip worth bearing in mind is to draw a light pencil line around the card about an inch and a half in from the edges all the way around. The area of card within this line is called the 'safe area' and this is ideally where lettering and other graphics displays should be concentrated. Anything outside this line is in danger of vanishing into the curved edges of the television screen when the recorded tape is played back.

What kind of letters should you use? Generally speaking, bold, simple typefaces work best, without fine lines or elaborate embellishments or serifs which the video camera will tend to lose when the picture is recorded. Most dry-print lettering is either white or black. Using white lettering is not only a better compromise for both titles, but you can always colour it afterwards to produce the kind of effect you want. If you are adding extra colours to your lettering, it's better to use pale, pastel shades, since the camera is happier with these colours. Deep colours like vivid reds, and harsh contrasts like blues and greens don't seem to produce as pleasing an effect when seen through a video camera as quieter combinations do.

Once your titles have been prepared, you can shoot each card separately for the right amount of time for the message to be absorbed. Ideally, the cards should be fixed to a vertical surface, with the camera set on its tripod at a height equal to the mid-point of the card, and aimed and focussed at this centre point. This guarantees that the horizontals and verticals will be straight lines, though you will have to check that the top and the bottom of the card is level. To light the card properly, you need one light on either side of the camera, of approximately equal power, and angled at about forty-five degrees to the paper. To avoid any tendency towards awkward reflections, position the lights slightly above the camera angled slightly downwards towards the paper.

As you continue to look through a succession of cards, it's a good idea if you make sure that the words on each card are in approximately the same place. This means that as you record each card in turn, with a cut to the next one, and the next, and so on, the progression will be fairly smooth rather than a succession of jump-cuts. If you find you have a lot of titles to record, you could even mount the cards in a frame or in a ring binder, so that all you have to do between shots is lift the top card out or flip over a sheet in the ring binder, to cut the recording time down to a minimum.

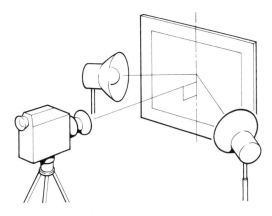

To shoot titles properly, the camera must be square on to the surface to prevent horizontals and verticals being distorted. This is easiest to arrange by mounting the title card on a vertical surface and aiming the camera at the mid-point of the card. Light it with two equal-intensity lamps arranged on either side of the camera but slightly above it (or below it) to avoid unwanted shadows or reflections.

Keep titles brief for maximum effect. It is better to split a lot of information over a series of cards. Use large letters in either solid or outline characters, and keep to simple, easily-read typefaces.

You can even record a set of credit titles scrolling up the screen by using what television producers had to use before graphics generators were invented. You draw out the titles on a long sheet of paper which is stuck down on the edge of a large-diameter drum which is mounted on a horizontal pivot, so that it can be turned very slowly. You stand the camera edge on to the drum, and focus it on the nearest point of the drum's circumference. All you then have to do is switch the camera to record as you rotate the drum slowly, and the titles mounted on its edge will scroll slowly up the screen.

Another idea which can link the titles more closely to the pro-gramme itself is to take a series of pictures with a stills camera while you're out on location shooting the programme. If you have the best of these enlarged to the same size as the graphic cards, you can use them as backgrounds to the titles. You can either write the credits in white on sheets of transparent gel, which you can mount one after the other in front of the photograph for a title sequence with the same picture. You can even build up a graph by putting different parts of it on different sheets of gel, and adding them in succession to the background photograph. Or you can use a series of pictures, one for each card of the titles, so that the picture changes every time the graphics change. In fact, you don't even need to take the pictures yourself. It's often possible to find pictures of the right kind of subject in the pages of glossy magazines or colour supplements which will do the job nearly as well.

One device which is often seen in television graphics is the title which is actually written on the screen as you watch. You can do this yourself by using a blackboard or a set of Letraset letters or even a set of children's lettered building blocks. Divide your title sequence up into a series of shots, each shot being as short as possible, and each time either add a single letter or even a short word, depending on the length of the shots and the overall speed at which you're aiming. If you can make these titles an integral part of your programme, so much the better. A title with building blocks would be perfect for a video of a child's birthday party; a title chalked on the wall would suit a documentary on a neighbourhood development scheme for example.

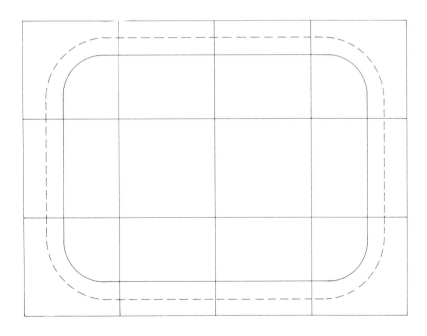

This diagram shows the proportions of the television screen – three units deep and four units wide. But because of the curvature of the screen, titles and graphics are best kept to the 'safe area' inside the lines. Title cards can be drawn smaller than screen size – 21 cm by 28 cm is ideal.

The more you can make your graphics part of the action, the better the effect will be. Let's say you want to shoot a video of a family game of beach cricket during the summer holidays. You can write the title in the sand before you start. You can even add names, details of the score and other comments as the action progresses, rather like the dialogue cards in silent movies. And with a little more preparation, the effects you produce could be completely professional. A title for the steam-railway programme we used as our example earlier in the book could be written out in Letraset in the style of a railway timetable. Placed over the original with a few pieces of Blu-Tack on the day while you shoot the title, particularly if there's plenty of steam drifting past, and a background of engine whistles and loudspeaker announcements, and you couldn't improve on that effect with all the technology in the world.

Finally, you can produce more ambitious graphics by using simple animation. If you build up a multi-layered title card, you can write some of the information on the top layer, then pull this top layer away (with your hands out of shot) to reveal another layer of information, and then another, and so on. You can mix drawings and words, so that a drawing of a train pulls on the title of the railway programme, or a car pulls away from the kerb, leaving the title 'The Journey' written on the road surface. Either way the only limit is your own artistic ability, and your originality, because it's often possible to assemble these pictures from photographs, line engravings, posters or other existing picture sources. All you need is a multi-layer construction, and hand grips which allow you to pull away different parts of the diagram smoothly and unobtrusively, with your hands out of shot the whole time.

Cards are a great deal easier to change if they are clipped into a ring binder. Each card can then be flipped over out of the way, to reveal the next are already in position.

Titles don't always have to be drawn on cards. Sometimes they can be added as part of the scenery, like letters chalked on a wall, for example.

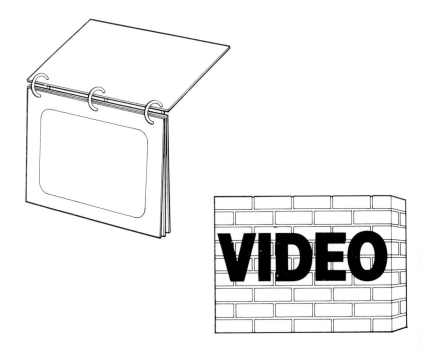

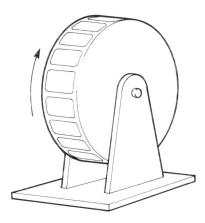

Two other ways of working with title cards – mounting them on an easel (left) or on the rim of a large drum (right) which is then turned slowly in front of the camera, so that the titles appear to move up the screen.

More and more modern cameras offer a clever little facility which makes it easier to produce top-quality graphics with a minimum of time and fuss. All you need is a card with either a title or a caption written on it, and perhaps a set of basic shapes like a rectangle or a circle in a contrasting colour to the background. Controls on the camera not only allow you to record several of these images in the camera's memory, but you can also select the colours in which you want the captions to be shown on the screen, and also instruct the camera to superimpose the captions or the shapes on the pictures you are actually recording. To take the beach cricket video, you can store a circle (representing a cricket ball) in the camera's memory, along with the title 'Seaside Test Match' on another frame in the memory. Then when you start shooting the match in progress, you can set the camera controls to call up the frame with the 'Seaside Test Match' title and press another button at the time you want the title to appear superimposed on the picture you are recording. Press the same button again, and the title disappears. You can then call up the frame with the circle on it, and start shooting from another angle. When you want to pause the action, or change to another part of the match, you press the titles button, and the picture is contained in a circle, until you cut to another picture and then remove the symbol. With the addition and removal of titles and graphics like this, and the use of still pictures and slides, which can be recorded and worked into the action in a similar way, and the use of the fade controls, you have a useful battery of effects at your fingertips.

SPECIAL EFFECTS –
AT A PRICE

Whenever we watch television, we can hardly help noticing the amazing variety of special effects which are brought to bear on everything from children's serials to promotional trailers. Some are picture effects – the picture you've been watching is rolled over, or flipped, or shrunk or flattened or distorted into all kinds of different shapes. Images can appear as part of other images, people can be made to appear as if they're part of a scene thousands of miles away – or they can be made to change, or talk to an identical self on the other side of the room, or disappear entirely. New pictures can be made to appear from nowhere – or from parts of the furniture, mirrors on the wall, or from the tiniest and most insignificant detail in the previous scene. Or, through the immensely powerful computer-graphics systems, they can be created entirely from the imagination of an artist, working throughout from electronics.

There's another kind of special-effects too, which is common to both television and feature films in the cinema. This is not so much involved with creating a new reality by electronic means, but by producing a convincing illusion of reality in optical terms. In other words, producing a severed limb for a horror movie, or a spaceship docking at a space station for a science fiction sequence, or a convincing explosion for a cops-and-robbers series – even when they're done with stuntmen, models, or controlled explosives and smoke-bombs, or by clever make-up and fake blood (called 'Kensington Gore'), they all count as special effects. In some cases, such as the 'Star Wars' series, the money spent on the ambitious special effects accounted for a large part of the budget – and rightly so, since the results accounted for a major part of the films' appeal.

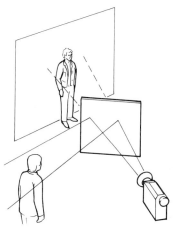

Many electronic special effects seen on television call for expensive and sophisticated equipment – but some (like one picture wiping another off the screen) can be carried out optically. All you have to do is set up the second shot in front of the camera in the usual way. Then arrange the subject of the first shot so that the camera sees it reflected in the mirror at the same focus setting as the second shot. Start recording, then pull the mirror smoothly sideways so the image of the first shot moves off camera to be replaced by the direct second shot.

Unfortunately, this is one area where the amateur programme-maker's resources are bound to be severely limited. Even simple dissolving from one image to another – a 'mix' – is well beyond the present state-of-the-art in video equipment, and it's likely to remain one area where video shooting lags behind ciné home-movies for some time to come. A simple dissolve on a movie camera can be done by a carefully preplanned double exposure, but there's no practical way of doing that inside the most expensive of video cameras. As things stand, mixes and dissolves can only be added in the sophisticated and expensive professional facilities where television programmes are edited.

But there are one or two useful tricks which can be made to work quite well, with a little ingenuity and pre-planning. A simple 'wipe' effect is a neat alternative to a mix, where instead of one picture dissolving into another, the new image simply wipes across the screen, blocking out the old one as it moves. This can be done with a large, good-quality mirror, provided the two scenes you want to use in your wipe effect are close enough together for the mirror trick to work.

Let's assume that you want to wipe from a distant background in one direction, to someone delivering a piece to camera against a different part of that background. You set up your camera with the mirror angled in front of it so that when looking through the viewfinder, all you see is the background reflected in the mirror, looking like a direct view of the scene itself – except that you will have to choose a shot where the left-right reversal produced by the mirror won't be obvious to the audience.

Then you move the mirror out of the way, leaving the camera locked in position on its tripod, and you pose the presenter in the right spot for the framing to be correct (remember, you can't move the camera) and far enough away for there to be no need to change the focus. Put the mirror back, adjusting the angle so that the framing of the reflected shot is as you want it, set the camera into the pause mode, then as you press the 'start' button, give the signal for the mirror to be slid sideways, slowly and smoothly and without changing the angle with the subject. As soon as your presenter sees the mirror clear the camera lens, he or she knows they're in shot, and they can start saying their piece. The most difficult part is getting the mirror movement right, so that shakiness or a change in the angle between subject mirror and camera doesn't give the game away – and some kind of mounting, where the mirror slides in a channeled piece of wood to act as a support might help here. But when done properly, it can be a surprisingly effective shot. And your audience can't help wondering how you achieved it.

Another special effect can be achieved with mirrors, but is really limited for title shots or more artistic or adventurous subjects. You need a set of three or four rectangular mirrors of identical size, which you can assemble into a tube of triangular section (rather like a Toblerone chocolate pack) or square section, which you place over the camera lens, so that it's looking down the tube from one end to the other. Shoot the subject through that and, depending on the size of the mirrors and the way you've framed the shot, you should end up with some interesting kaleidoscopic effects, particularly with very colourful or very active subjects.

You can also experiment with a form of animation. If you fit the camera on a tripod and tighten up all the adjustments, it should stay perfectly fixed relative to the landscape. If you then record a few

frames at a time – down to a fraction of a second or so per shot if your camera will allow this – you can magnify any natural or deliberate changes in the landscape by spacing your recordings accordingly. You can see the tide come in to cover a beach in a few seconds, a car park fill, and empty in about the same time, weather change from sun to rain, or sunshine deepen into twilight or darkness. All these things can be made to serve a purpose in telling a story, as well as being clever and intriguing shots in their own right. They can suggest the passing of time or a change of mood – particularly in the case of the weather shot – or even, with a careful choice of subject, something more challenging, sinister, or funny.

This kind of time-lapse shot can also be made to work as an integral part of the action, by setting up your own action to treat in this way. The loading of an enormous amount of luggage into the boot of a car, the painting of a wall, the tidying up of a room – all can be made to happen by magic by concentrating on the changes and omitting any human figures altogether. You could try adding a person or two as an experiment – ask them to freeze their positions whenever you record that fraction of a second for each shot, but between shots they can and should move as much as they like.

Some cameras have an optional remote control unit which can help to make these animated sequences a lot easier. If the camera is securely mounted on a tripod and set up with the focus and framing correct, you can record a series of half-second shots of the surroundings using a special 'animation' button, and then press the start/stop button on the remote control unit every time you want to record one of these 'snapshots'. Once you have reached the end of the animated sequence, all you need do is press the 'animation' button again, and the camera reverts to normal operation.

You can even extend this kind of effect into more conventional animation, using plasticine figures whose shape can be changed shot by shot, or even children's toys whose arms and legs can be bent into position. Your only limitation is the time you have available, your own ingenuity, and the shortest shot your camera will allow you to record, even by overlapping one shot with the next to cut down the length of shots still further. But there is a way of being able to use this effect and several others: buying or borrowing a small movie camera, shooting a scene on film, and then copying the result on to tape. Because film cameras can be made to shoot frame by frame, smooth animation is much easier – and you can even shoot dissolves between different scenes, and slow-motion subjects too.

To make use of these effects in your video production, you need to re-record the processed film sequences on your video camera, at the right place in the programme. This means using a projector –

preferably one with the facility to play back at 16 2/3 or 25 frames per second (1/3 or 1/2 of the television and video rate) rather than the more common 18 and 24 frames per second used for film work. As you're going to have to edit each extract on to your programme tape as another shot, you'll need to make sure everything is running properly, and that both projector and camera are correctly focussed, before you start recording. To reduce distortion to the minimum, stand the camera and the projector side by side, with the screen on to which you're projecting the film set at right angles to both of them. Adjust the framing, with the projector running, so that you capture most of the picture in the video viewfinder, though you're bound to lose a little of it because film cameras have a differently-shaped frame.

It's also helpful to have some kind of warning of the start of the sequence you want to record. It's easy enough to splice any film sequence in front of your special effects shot to act as a leader – either a blank film with the count-down in seconds to the start of your own piece of film, or another shot with a clearly identifiable end to it, as a warning that your shot is about to follow it at the vital instant. A shot of someone diving into a swimming pool would be ideal, with the cut to your recording made at the moment they hit the water, giving you an unmistakable cue to press the 'start' button.

There are more elaborate setups you can use to create an illusion of reality – many of them easier than you might think. For example, the deep space sequences showing enormously complicated space vehicles manoeuvring against a starlit background, and hanging without any visible means of support, are simple to stage. You need some convincing models, made from modified plastic kits and all kinds of oddments from margarine containers to press studs, painted in the right kind of colours and with a mass of small and complex detail to hit at a large construction a long way away. These are supported on stands which are painted matt black, so that they don't reflect the light, and they're arranged in front of a black background sheet, pierced with a pattern of holes to suggest a vast starscape from lights hidden behind the sheet. The lighting on the model has to be done carefully, so that it's quite subdued and casts deep shadows, as it would from a single star or planet close enough to illuminate the scene – a single light should do the trick, but angle it so that it doesn't show up the stand.

We've concentrated so far on visual special effects – but any scene can be made much more convincing with the right kind of sound track. But if the right effect isn't readily available, you can do an awful lot by playing tricks on your microphone, and making a sound which is close enough to the original to fool your audience. How many people know you can make the rubbing together of two sandpaper blocks sound like the approach of a steam train? Or that squashing a half-empty bag of flour with the right rhythm sounds

Experimenting with animation is effective and great fun to do.

99

like footsteps in deep snow? Or that you can use a vacuum cleaner to simulate the subdued whistle of jet engines?

Weather sound effects are always useful. Falling rain can be concocted by placing your microphone underneath a paper chute which then has castor sugar trickled down it steadily. Your story calls for heavier rain – a tropical downpour, perhaps? Hold a large sieve over your microphone, drop a couple of dozen dried peas into the sieve and roll them backwards and forwards. Wind? Draw a piece of silk across a wooden grating. Rustling of the trees? Rattle a handful of magnetic tape in front of the microphone. These are just a few of the tricks you can try. Like all special effects, they depend on ingenuity and invention, and hopefully these few examples will have whetted your appetite to try other ways to create the effects you want for your own programmes.

THE SCRIPT

Chapter 10

Turning a script into pictures. Here's a beautifully restored station booking hall – but the pictures must match the words, so either the shot needs more people in it, or the script needs amending to make some reference to the peace and quiet before the crowds arrive.

The engine backs onto the train. Try to capture the moment when the engine and coaches meet.

For many people, producing the script is the most daunting part of making a video programme. Something about the very idea of scriptwriting makes it sound challenging and dramatic – the kind of image which conjures up Scott Fitzgerald or Dennis Potter, turning out a masterpiece for the large or small screen. But that's like saying all cars are Rolls Royce, or all paintings are Picassos. Every programme ever made had to have a script; the script might exist on the back of an envelope, on a laundry bill or entirely in the producer's head, but the truth remains that precious few programmes would ever be completed unless someone, somewhere, had an idea of what it was trying to say, and how it was going to try to say it.

So let's approach this matter of scriptwriting, as we've tried to approach every other part of the art of programme-making so far: let's follow the professionals in how they approach their tasks, but let's keep it simple in keeping with our objectives. As with everything else, once you've proved you can write a simple script or make a simple programme, developing your ideas and your techniques so that you can turn out work which is more ambitious and more successful is much less daunting a prospect.

The first thing to decide is what kind of script we're talking about. To make a complex programme, there has to be a whole series of scripts. There's a dialogue script, for any dramatised sequences in the programme, there's the presenter's script to tell him what he has to say to camera, and when he has to say it, there's a sound script to lay down all the details of how the different sound tracks are to be mixed and balanced to make the finished programme sound-track. Then there are interview scripts to set out the questions to be put to the presenters and, once the interviews had been recorded, the quotes which will be used out of the answers they gave to those questions. There will also be a commentary script, for the voice-over which will be recorded to the edited programme and, since professional programmes are very rarely shot in the same order as they're edited, there will be a shooting script to tell the production crew, the artistes and the director the order in which the different shots will actually be recorded. Finally, there's the programme script which will tie all these different bits of information together as the master specification to which the programme will actually be made.

It makes sense to start with the programme script, as that provides the basic framework for the programme, and everything else has to be fitted to it. Now don't forget this can be as simple, or as complicated, as you want it to be. Its primary function is to give you a chance to decide what you want your programme to do, and how you propose to set about making it. So let's begin with the preserved-railway example we looked at earlier in the book.

What's the story of the programme to be? A day at the So-and-So Steam Railway? A journey along the line from end to end? A look at what dedicated volunteers have been able to achieve in keeping open a line that was given up for lost when it closed more than twenty years ago? A simple sequence of trains arriving and departing at a busy station, and a look at the kind of people who come here for a day out? Each of these approaches could be a perfectly valid reason for a programme, and each of them would demand a slightly different approach from each of the others.

For example, a simple look at the line from the end to end would involve round trips on one or more of the trains, with perhaps a pause or two en route to look at the people and places along the length of the route. A look at what the volunteers had achieved might start with similar sequences, but it would tend to stop to talk to the people who restored and run the railway – and it might include a sequence or two of people undertaking some of the heavy work which is needed to keep it going, year in and year out.

Another question worth asking is, what kind of audience is it intended for? A programme on a railway subject may be intended for young railway enthusiasts. If it's intended to be shown to people with no initial interest in the subject, it will be a different kind of programme – if it's meant for people old enough to remember the old steam trains with nostalgia, it will be a different kind of programme again. And all these factors affect what kind of script you produce.

So, let's begin. First of all, what are we going to make a programme about? It's a good idea to ask yourself a couple of questions about any possible subject before going any further. First of all, is it a subject you feel strongly about? Secondly, is it a subject that interests you? If the answer to either is 'yes' (preferably both), let's stop to consider the impact on your audience. You may be an absolute fanatic about breeding begonias, and if your audience is the local gardening club, you may be on to a winner with a programme on exactly that subject. But if your audience is the local rugby club, the percentage of begonia buffs among them may be very small indeed. So ask yourself two more questions – does it inform? In the railway example we looked at, the answer should certainly be yes. Does it entertain? That really depends on the way in which you treat the subject – which comes next.

It's important to remember two things above all. People are interested in the extraordinary, the unexpected and the surprising far more than the predictable. This is why you always need to be on the lookout for the unexpected shot, and the surprising or illuminating fact to put in the programme. But television, or video for that matter, can't compete with the printed page for putting over a sheer mass of detailed information. You need to confine yourself to the most important facts that will serve your purpose in making the programme. And that means thinking, planning, and very often doing your homework, and a little research as well.

If we're still talking about the railway subject, any facts and figures about the railway will be useful. Ask yourself the kind of questions an inquisitive visitor might ask, and if you don't know the answer, then ask someone else: that's research. When was it first built? When was it closed? How did they manage to get it reopened? When did they start? What kind of work did they have to do to get the trains running? Where did the engines and coaches come from? How many passengers do they carry in a year? How many volunteers work on the line? What kind of people are they? How many trains a day do they run at the height of the season? Does the line make a profit? What are they planning to do next? And when? It's questions like these, and others like them, which constitute programme research – and the answers should go into your script, and into your programme.

How are you going to find these answers? Some might come from reference books – others from specialist journals like, in this case, railway-enthusiast magazines. But another good idea is to pay a visit in person, to do a recce – not only can you talk to people, and collect valuable information, but you can also look for good subjects for shots, without at this stage carting your camera about and recording them. Think in terms of sequences at this stage, and when you get home, consult your notes to work out a treatment – a sketch of how the finished programme will fit together, with the picture sequences written down the left-hand side of the page, and the words on the right. Something like this, in fact, with a succession of one-line points you want to make:

PICTURE:	SOUND:
1 Crowds queuing in booking office.	Commentary: Why are so many people queuing up to spend money on a ride on a train?
2 Engine backing on to train.	Because it's a steam train on a private railway – nothing to do with British Rail.
3 Driver and fireman in cab.	Every man here is an unpaid volunteer.
4 Interview driver.	Wonderful to be working on steam engine again – nothing like them –more like living creature than piece of machinery.
5 Guard looks at watch.	Completely professional organisation – everything run on strict timetable.
6 Signalman pulling levers.	Almost time for train to leave.

| 7 Train departs. | Train leaves – but fact that trains are running at all along this line is due to years of heavy work by people from all walks of life. |
| 8 Vox-Pops volunteers. | What they do for a living – what they do on the railway – what it involves, and why they enjoy doing it. . . . |

You can use a treatment to check your thinking, to spot possible weak points in that thinking, and to see where extra shots or sequences of shots might be needed. You can even use it to produce a rough timing for the programme – as a rule of thumb, each of the points in the SOUNDS column should take a rough average of fifteen seconds each. So on these eight sequences so far, there are sixteen points altogether, which add up to 240 seconds, or 4 minutes. You could add a little more for the vox-pops in sequence eight, depending on the range of different people you found to talk to, another ten seconds or so for the opening titles and the start of the programme, and say another 30 seconds for the departure of the train, which is going to be interesting enough in its own right to do without any of the commentary. Which all adds up to a total of about 5 minutes – and a 20-minute programme is going to involve about four times as much material as this.

Once you've got the treatment properly worked out, you can use that as a framework for the programme script proper. All it needs is an expansion of the one-line points outlined above, with more detailed notes on the kind of shots you're looking for to do justice to the words. But in turning notes into a proper commentary, it's worth bearing one or two more points in mind.

The first requirement is clarity; the second is simplicity. Remember that your audience is not going to be reading your words, or the words of any of your contributors – they're going to be hearing them. Keep the sentences short, keep the words and phrases simple, let the pictures tell the story. Don't tell the audience about what they can already see for themselves on the screen – use the commentary to tell them all the background facts which the pictures can't convey.

It's a useful idea to read out the words you've written for the commentary. You don't want a breathless commentary from the start of the programme to the finish without a break. Establish a gentler pace, with room for the action and the sound effects to help the story along on their own. Some scriptwriters say a ratio of about two minutes of words to every three minutes of programme is the right kind of ratio to aim at – but this will probably vary a little from subject to subject.

So far, we've been talking about subjects which are scripted before they're shot. In that sense, the job of the script is to tell your audience about the subject you've chosen in the same way as you might tell them yourself, face to face. Just as appearing in front of the camera requires that you treat it as a friend, to be informed and entertained, so your script should treat the audience in the same way. Surprise them, inform them, entertain them – as clearly and as economically as you can, reinforcing the pictures and the messages THEY carry rather than repeating them in words. Learn to think in terms of picture sequences to match the words you give your presenter or your commentary – work to a treatment which sets out what the programme will do, in words or pictures, from start to finish.

But be careful never to become the slave of your script. No matter how carefully you research the subject, no matter how often you visit the locations before shooting begins, and no matter how long you spend talking to contributors before you interview them, there are ALWAYS surprises waiting, once you start to make your programme. Be flexible, and learn to respond to changes by changing your script, and your approach where necessary. Learn to see surprises, not as hostile events which undo your careful preparation, but as opportunities to make an even better programme. In a documentary, a new shift in the subject can make your programme more topical – in a drama, a change of weather or in a location may give you the chance to take advantage of it, to build the change into the story in some way.

Of course, some programmes can't start with a script in this way. Treatments which depend on actual events being recorded as accurately as possible may not be predictable enough for a full script to begin with. In those cases, produce as flexible a treatment as you can from the research you've been able to do – even if you don't know exactly how a contest or event will finish, you must know what you want your programme to say, and this must influence how you approach the programme. So work out what parts of the subject you will be shooting, in which order, and then keep your eyes open for any change in circumstances which may mean a new angle. Once the programme is shot, you can then write the script, safe in the knowledge that all you now have to do is explain what the audience won't know from simply watching the pictures.

It's difficult to think of enough examples to cover all the different kinds of programme subject which fall into this category. One possibility might be some local sporting derby between two neigh-bouring villages – say, a cricket match or a tug-of-war – where the history of previous events in the series has established a clear favourite and an equally clear outsider. Your finished script will obviously depend on who finally wins the contest you're shooting – so you can't write it beforehand. All you can do is postpone the creative decisions which depend on which team wins, until you actually know.

So the treatment might be drawn up with a look at both villages, and a few vox-pop interviews about the importance (or the irrel-evance) of the event to most of the inhabitants. Then you could look at some of the more interesting characters from both teams, at their backgrounds, at what they feel about the contest, and about their opponents. By the time the event is ready to begin, you can select your shots to heighten the drama of the contest, by looking for anything which suggests that THIS year, perhaps the outsiders will overturn the predictions being made – whichever way the result eventually goes, the will-they-won't-they quality of a possible vic-tory against the odds is bound to hold your audience's interest.

This quality can be heightened afterwards, when you DO write the script in the light of the final result. On the day, your priorities are to capture anything which stresses the closeness of the contest, the anxiety of the competitors, and the possibility that either side may win. The longer the result is in doubt, the better for your programme – from your point of view, the worst possible result is an early victory for the favourites.

If this should happen have a contingency plan ready. Make the most of the early stages of the contest. Capture the announcement of the result, and then concentrate on the emotions of the losers. Why DO they feel the event is so predictable? Could their approach to the contest be at fault? What are they going to do to make next year a different story – and so on. On the other hand, if the outsiders DO win, then some of those questions will need to be put to the losing favourites, in between concentrating on the joy and surprise of the victory. Ask some of the experts why this change in fortunes happened this year. And after it's all over, ask the inhabi-tants of the winning village whether they now feel the same about the event as before.

Depending on the outcome of the contest, you will now end up with a finished programme, apart from the script. Your audience will see two places, interviews with people in those places, interviews with people preparing for a sporting event, shots of the event itself, with one team being announced as the winners, wild jubilation on one side and disappointment on the other, then some more inter-views to round the whole thing off. All that's needed is an expla-nation of where we are, what's happening and who's talking – and there's your script.

Shots like this, showing the
engine crew, can play a logical
part in the sequence.

Or, as here, they can be used
to carry quotes from the driver
on the sound track while the
picture shows him at work,
rather than in the artificial and
often intimidating set-up of a
formal interview.

Look for other pointers to
imminent departure, such as
the signal arm dropping to
:show 'clear' ...

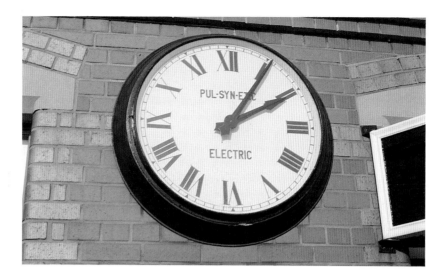

... and the station clock at the departure time.

The guard waves his green flag to signal the driver to start . . .

And finally the train leaves.

Of course, there's a little more to it than that. Professional programme makers can afford the luxury of editing to a finished script, where the subject and the approach merit it, but in most cases this is impossible for the home video producer. Having to edit in the camera means the script will need to be added afterwards, if only to make up for differences in the lengths of shots, or in the way sequences turn out on the day, compared with the plans included in the treatment. Just about the only exception to this is when you're shooting a play, to a scripted dialogue, where ALL the words are laid down in advance, and the whole programme hinges on the script. In all other programmes, the script – or the final version of it at least – is going to come last.

Let's imagine now that you're at that stage. To make the example slightly more straightforward, we'll go back to the railway example we were looking at earlier. From the treatment, you can see that in the opening section of the programme, there are likely to be six pieces of script: the first one about fifteen seconds long, the next thirty seconds, the third fifteen seconds and leading to an interview with the engine driver, the fourth and fifth fifteen seconds apiece, and leading to the departure of the train, and the final section thirty seconds, leading to a series of vox-pop interviews with the volunteers who helped to re-open the line and are helping to keep it open.

Now you have the edited sequence of shots making up the programme, you can check those estimated times, to see how much room you have for each section of the script. Generally speaking, people reading a script average between two and a half and three words a second, which means 150 to 180 words a minute. So the first point in your treatment may have to cover a crowds shot which, after a pause to establish itself because it's the start of the programme, actually lasts for twenty seconds – in other words, 50 to 60 words. So start off with something along the lines of the point in the treatment, which actually relates to the pictures you shot. In this case we'll assume there were three shots of the booking office with people paying money, the clerk issuing tickets and the crowds on the platform, in that order.

The first question to ask yourself is 'What's unusual about what we're seeing? It isn't people paying money for train tickets, nor people queuing to hand over their money at that. It isn't the crowds on the platforms either – it's the combination of all these things with the holiday clothes and holiday atmosphere. So what we need is something along the lines of:

'What is it that makes people queue up to hand over hard-earned money for a ride on a train? Not to get to work, not to make some urgent and special journey to the other end of the country – but just as a way of spending a pleasant holiday afternoon with the rest of the family'. That amounts to 57 words – just about right for the first section, covering the subject of the shots in the right order.

Now to the second section. Here again, we have three shots – the coaches waiting in the platform with people climbing aboard, the engine backing on to the head of the train, and a panning shot up to the crest on the side of the tender. The sequence lasts for just 22 seconds – equivalent to between 55 and 66 words of script. So here goes, once again: 'It's certainly a popular idea – there's precious few seats to spare on any of the trains (*over the crowded coaches in the platform*). But no-one seems to mind, for this is a very different kind of railway – it's privately run, and all the trains are hauled by beautifully restored steam engines (*over the engine backing on to the train*). It's a colourful trip back into the past, and it's absolutely nothing to do with British Rail. . . .' (*Pan to the old railway's crest on the tender, emphasising the lack of connection with British Rail*). The total – 62 words – is once again the right kind of length to do justice to the pictures.

On to the third sequence. A shorter shot of the driver and fireman on the footplate getting ready for departure, followed by a close-up of the driver, which links into the interview which follows. Total time 12 seconds – or between 30 and 36 words. This time, because it links into an interview which has already been recorded, you need to check who the interviewee is, and what his first words were. It turns out the driver is called Fred Jones, and he begins his interview with the words 'It's wonderful to be working with steam engines again – they're more like living things than pieces of machinery'. So your piece of script has three objectives. It must have between 30 and 36 words, it must introduce Fred Jones, and it must link smoothly into his first words.

Once again, let's keep an eye on the surprising and the unexpected. 'Every person working here is a volunteer, and none of them is paid a penny for the work they put in. But for ex-British rail driver Fred Jones, working at a job he loved is ample compensation'. As a piece, it does introduce the driver, and it links to his opening words, but at 38 words, it's a fraction too long. How can we shorten it? If we simplify and shorten the first sentence into two, so that they now read 'Every person working here is a volunteer. No-one earns a penny for their work', we save six whole words – enough to make the piece fit.

Scriptwriting is a kind of puzzle, fitting words into exact spaces, to meet very precise demands. It means timing everything around your spoken word.

A SIMPLE
DOCUMENTARY

Chapter 11

Now that we've covered most of the different areas where a little more care and a little more thought can help you produce a more professional programme, let's now look at how those ideas can be put into practice in a series of different case studies. In this chapter, and the following three chapters, we're going to look at a quartet of different programme subjects. We'll start with the documentary, since this in many ways the most straightforward type of subject, and the one which most programme-makers begin with. But first, we need to take some decisions as to what kind of subject the programme should cover.

Family holidays are one of the most common subjects for home videos – sometimes, once the novelty of seeing themselves on the screen has worn off, they might only be of marginal interest to members of the family and close friends or relatives, and for anyone else they're likely to be instant boredom. So what can we do to take a hackneyed subject like this and make it a little bit more interesting, to whoever might be watching?

Professionals often say that if a subject is interesting, then it should make good television. That isn't always true, since some subjects can be extremely interesting without being very visual – but it isn't a bad starting point. Others say you should go for the unusual – if your audience is watching something which isn't familiar or routine or predictable, then they'll enjoy what they see. And a third piece of advice is to concentrate on things changing – where there's change, and movement, then a programme shouldn't be dull.

Apply this to the family holiday, and it's clear that one potential subject is in the journey by which you reach your chosen holiday spot. If it's abroad, and in an out-of-the-way place, and if you're going by car or train rather than by air, then you've several more factors in your favour – though a good programme-maker should be able to do a lot with a bus trip to Blackpool. Like everything, planning, and an ever-open eye for the unusual is vital.

So we've decided on recording a family drive to Spain as the subject of our documentary. Now comes the first of an almost endless series of decisions which lie between you and the finished programme. Does the first shot show the loaded car pulling away from the family home? Or do you plan to show some of the preparations? Family chats about where to go and how to book and all

the other preliminaries to the holiday might be lethal to the programme's audience appeal – what you should be thinking about is
some unexpected twist, so that the programme starts with a surprise
which the audience didn't expect.

What about starting your programme part way along the journey?
And without showing the family at all? You might set up your camera
at the first photogenic pavement cafe after you disembark from the
cross-Channel ferry. Brief the rest of the family on what they have to
do, then set up your camera and shoot some of the local colour –
people drinking coffee, buying long sticks of French bread, a busy
and colourful street market if you can find it. Once you've established the professional travelogue atmosphere, which you can
heighten afterwards with a piece of deadpan script in travel-
programme style, give the family the cue and let the loaded family
car suddenly appear in this piece of totally French townscape. The
sudden shift in your attention, and the appearance of familiar faces
in an unexpected context, should give your audience fair warning
that this is no boring family holiday-video, but something which has
taken a lot more thought.

Now we need a story – some kind of theme to carry the programme along, and to involve the audience in the family's experience. Some kind of conflict between different members of the party
over what route to follow, or where to make the first night stop,
might be one possibility. Or one member's obsession with food or
drink might add an ingredient of gentle comedy. If the rest of the
party is split between two cars, then something of a contest between
the two parts of the party to be the first to the destination, could
introduce a touch of drama and of tension. The decision is yours,
and there are many more ways in which the subject could be
treated.

Whichever approach you eventually choose, there are some
drawbacks you and your family should always be aware of. Programme making is a time-consuming occupation, and recording a
trip like this is going to make it take a lot longer than it would
otherwise have done. The easier your schedule, the better. And the
more you can involve the family and other members of the party in
what you're doing, and why, the more readily they'll accept the
reasons for any delays. To make any treatment work, you'll need a
lot of passing shots to emphasise the overseas locations, the different stages of the journey, and the changes in the surroundings as
you go further south. For each one, you'll need to stop and set up
your camera gear, they'll have to retreat up the road and come past
you after a pre-arranged time interval to allow you to be ready to
record their approach. And if anything goes wrong – your framing
isn't as it should be, someone walks in front of you as the car comes
around the corner, or whatever, they'll have to go back and run

through the whole thing again. Only when the shot is as you want it can they come back to collect you and your equipment and you can all resume your journey again.

Another possibility is to ask different members of the party what they expect the trip to be like, and what they're looking forward to most – and least – about it. Then you can ask them at intervals during the trip, either in the car when passing through unusual or spectacular scenery, when tucking into a sumptuous meal or when enjoying a coffee or a glass of wine under a sunshade in a pavement cafe, how the trip is living up to their expectations, or their forebodings. You could even try an interview-on-the-move with one of the drivers in the party, about the differences, and the difficulties which result from having to drive on the right-hand side of the road.

By being able to edit the shots on to the finished programme in a different order from the order in which they are recorded, you can make the statements more pointed, more dramatic or more humorous – someone saying beforehand that they are looking forward to all the sunshine in Spain before the trip starts could be followed by a shot of the same person standing in an obviously Spanish location and pulling a face while the rain pours down, and so on.

You can concentrate on more ambitious set-pieces whenever you meet an interruption in the journey. This at least means that the kind of mechanical breakdown, from a puncture to a more difficult problem, could be subject matter for your camera – though the co-operation of the rest of the party may tend to wear a little thin in conditions like this. Better to concentrate on happier reasons for pausing – the lunch, or the evening meal. Make each one an opportunity for 'fly-on-the-wall' techniques, shooting what people say, how they choose what to eat, how they react to it when it arrives, the conversation around the table afterwards.

When you stop for the night, remember that the kind of accommodation you find could be of genuine interest to anyone watching the programme, who may be making a similar journey in the future. Take a look around the hotel – a shot of the family round the swimming pool, the restaurant and the bars, and the decor and the furnishings in the rooms. But don't go for empty shots of static rooms if you can help it. A few energetic children making up for hours of being cooped up in a car by splashing about in the pool, or the drivers unwinding over an aperitif in the bar, or even the cases being unpacked in one of the rooms gives you a chance to mention standards, choices and prices. If you feel like taking a break from programme-making – and even professionals don't work ALL the time – then close on a shot which says 'Goodnight' (perhaps the younger members of the party wandering slowly up the stairs) and fade to black. Next morning you can fade up from black to your first shot, perhaps being ready for departure in the car-park, perhaps a Continental breakfast in the dining room, and your audience will understand that we're into the start of a new day.

What happens when we reach journey's end? This is the most difficult part of the project for which to suggest examples, since everything will depend on the treatment you chose at the beginning, and on the way the trip has developed so far. But try, as you did at the beginning, to opt for the surprise, the unexpected and – hopefully – the interesting. If one of the party is a car fanatic, whose reaction to the safe arrival at your destination is to disappear beneath the car to check that all is well, he's worth his weight in gold. It's a theme you could well follow up, looking at each of the members of the party making for whatever they feel makes the holiday, and the journey to it, worthwhile.

For one member of the family, it could be eyeing-up the girls outside the local disco, for another it could be a chic cocktail bar, for the younger ones it could be the beach or the funfair, and for the older ones the boutiques or the local market. You could end your programme with a sequence of colourful shots of each member of the family heading for his or her favourite spot or pastime, and you could try overlaying each shot with a few words from that particular person on what they enjoy about the place. And your final shot – something that rounds off the holiday, the journey and the story in a single graphic image. The choice, once again, has to be up to you, but one possibility might be the driver looking fondly at the car which brought the family all this way to their holiday. The rest of the group are making their way into town, the sun is setting over the beach and the evening beckons – but he turns back, as an afterthought, and gives the bonnet a gentle pat, before rushing after the other members of the party.

Or you could be slightly more ambitious. Having spent all that time and trouble to get here, you could make the place itself the subject of another programme. This time, as you have the luxury of no travelling to do until it's time to set off for home, you can concentrate on a new treatment, and a full recce by way of research, before you have to shoot anything. Look around the place for anything which catches your eye as programme material – interesting people, unusual sights, surprises of every kind. Remember, the kind of subjects which interest and entertain you, as a visitor, are likely to interest your audience too, particularly if you shoot them with a fresh, imaginative approach.

There's another option open to you now you have an on-the-spot location. You can use another member of the family – or yourself, if someone else can operate the camera – as a presenter. This might help in bringing some scenes to life – but take care. It can be easier in most cases to shoot sequences without people over-reacting to your presence if you remain unobtrusive: so if you do use a presenter, don't overuse him or her. Keep some scenes as pure actuality – locals haggling at the fruit and vegetable stall, a needle match of boules in the village square, fishing boats landing their catches in the harbour. When you have a long enough sequence to establish the scene, then you can bring in your presenter if you have something definite to say.

By the end of your holiday, you should have two things to take back with you. The first is a pair of programmes, on the journey and on your destination, which will act as a powerful memory of this holiday trip during all the cold, dark winter evenings to come. But keep things in proportion. Ration the number of days on which you actually shoot in case, for you, the holiday becomes just another assignment. Make sure that the other thing you take with you on the return trip is a feeling of being rested and refreshed, and not overworked.

A low angle shot, emphasising the natural patterns of this scene.

SHOOTING AN EVENT

Chapter 12

In this chapter, we're about to look in slightly more detail at the ins and outs of covering an event which is happening anyway, and where your recording it as the subject of a video programme is an additional bonus. This means that the little set-pieces we discussed in the previous chapter are going to be mainly impossible. You may have the chance to set up some individual shots by seizing the opportunity to ask for people's co-operation, but generally speaking the priorities of the event itself are going to rule this out, apart from occasional exceptions. And they will depend on the nature of the subject.

But what IS the subject? We looked earlier at two examples of covering events on video – the carnival procession, and the local sporting derby. Now we'll switch our attention to a third example, which must be one of the most common subjects for a family video – a wedding. Now there is already a sizeable industry which makes a living from producing wedding videos to order; but unless you and the official video producer actually get in each other's way, there's no reason why you can't both make your different versions of the great event, and comparisons might be to your advantage. Remember that, to the professional, this is just another wedding – so the chances are he will be applying a standard formula which leaves out all the worries and all the effort of trying to produce something totally individual. You, on the other hand, should be approaching it as a challenge, using every opportunity to make it an interesting, entertaining and involving record of a very special day.

Having said that, of course, you don't need to confine your shooting to the day itself. Your biggest advantage over the professional wedding-video maker, who's working to a very tight schedule, is that if it's a wedding in your immediate family you're likely to have access to the people and the locations for all the preparations. Very few weddings involve just the day itself, as a spur-of-the-moment decision – most of them are the results of weeks of effort, even more planning than a video programme, and a number of problems and crises which threaten the success of the whole event, but which are usually resolved well in time for all to go off successfully.

So the first step, as before, is to decide what your starting point should be. Unless there's genuine acting talent in the family, it's probably better not to ask the happy couple to restage the moment of the proposal and the acceptance. Try to find some other way of making the point – perhaps a shot in the living room of the bride's parents sorting through catalogues of printed invitations, the seating plan and menus for the reception, prices for taxis and all the rest of the preparatory paperwork. Your introductory shot probably won't give the game away on its own, so keep the audience guessing for a while – then tilt the camera down to a newspaper lying on the table. Cut to a close-up of the page, showing the wedding announcements with the one relating to the wedding which is the subject of the video being circled for emphasis.

You can cover the preparations in one of two ways. You can either record the discussions backwards and forwards, but there's the danger these could go on too long, and people could become too self-conscious. As most people know, from weddings in their own families, much of what's involved, all you really need is a suggestion of frantic activity with a touch of humour now and again. If you've got an insert-edit facility on your camera, you could shoot, say, five minutes of the discussion around what kind of invitation cards to order, who's going to sit next to who else at the reception, how many taxis will be needed and so on. Then any other shots you can capture later on, like the bride being fitted for her dress, or the groom's stag party (or the early stages of it at least) can be added afterwards as overlay shots using the insert-edit facility – because the sound-track of the discussion will carry on throughout, this will lend the other shots a slightly unearthly, dreamlike quality. (Remember, the overlay shots added with insert edit don't replace the original soundtrack).

Here again, the option of editing afterwards does give you the chance of all kinds of links and contrasts – perhaps a shot of the bride being fitted for the dress, or a shot of the rehearsal linking directly to her arrival at the church and the procession down the aisle on the day itself.

As the day draws nearer, you may be able to film the rehearsals of the ceremony itself, and the responses. You can either record these straight, or you could do a little bit of interviewing – how the happy couple and the parents feel about the approaching ordeal. Will they remember what to say when? Will the best man lose the ring? Will the bride's father remember not to say anything when officially giving his daughter away? And what does the minister himself feel about weddings – dull routine, an assembly-line process, or every one different? What kind of things can go wrong – and have gone wrong at weddings which he's carried out?

Most wedding videos concentrate in great detail on the arrival of each of the guests at the church or registry office – but if you find the 'official' video will be doing that anyway, you might try picking a particular moment in the rehearsal, with say the bride and her father starting their walk down the aisle to the groom and the best man, waiting at the far end, then fade quickly to black. On the day itself, make sure you can stand in the same position (part of the research which you should be carrying out beforehand), and when the bride and her father reach a similar spot on their way into the church, fade up from black and start recording. You've covered the passing of time in a neat link which avoids all the cars and guests arriving and marching up the path before the ceremony itself begins.

One of the problems of shooting in a church, rather than in a registry office, is that a church is usually much darker. Introducing lights would be obtrusive, and may well not be allowed, so if you are able to go along to a rehearsal, use this as an opportunity to check out areas where the light is better than average, and check which places you will be able to use as camera positions on the day itself. Ideally, you want to be able to cover the arrival of the bride and her father, and the faces of all the principals in the ceremony, as well as of the minister who is conducting the proceedings. So a position to one side of the church, and opposite the altar steps is ideal – but watch out for the light from windows behind any of the principals turning them into mysterious silhouettes.

But when it comes to recording the actual ceremony, you have to ask yourself the question which must arise somewhere in the making of every programme. What is it the audience will be interested to see? Not every detail of the ceremony – we've all been to weddings and we know roughly what goes on – but perhaps the highlights like the vows, the question inviting anyone with 'just cause or impediment' to come forward and declare his or her objections, and the pronouncement of the couple as man and wife. It will demand some careful decisions as to where you should fade to black and fade up again as an indication of the passing of time, and it's a good idea to relieve the concentration on the group at the head of the aisle with some cutaways of the details of the church interior, or some of the faces of the guests, watching with rapt attention.

You can end the coverage inside the church with the departure of the couple to sign the register, and move into position for the photographs at the porch. The procedure inside a registry office would be much briefer, and you might think it worthwhile to record most of the words, while always being on the lookout for cutaways, close-ups of the register being signed, and so on. But here too, the end of the ceremony and the signing of the register give you your cue to move outside and be ready for the photographs.

Here you can follow a completely different policy from everyone else who is busy taking pictures for all they're worth. Because you deal in moving pictures, you shouldn't be competing with the snapshots in any case. You can be busy picking out the brief little close-ups which will act as an even more powerful means of recalling the day itself – the bride's mother suppressing a tear, the bride adjusting her veil, the groom and best man striking a pose for the photographer, the marshalling of the different groups of families and relatives. It's all very vivid and evocative stuff, and there's another way of tying it all up into a professional sequence for those with a camera which can produce insert edits.

After the wedding and the arrival of the official photographs, see if you can borrow a set of colour prints. Set them up in your 'studio', and edit each one for two or three seconds on to the part of the tape where you've recorded that actual photo being taken. This won't affect the sound-track, but an extra effect you could add over each of the still-photo edits, using the audio dub button, is the sound of an empty camera being cocked and then the shutter released. It's an effect often used on television, and it works well if you can get the timing of the sound effect exactly right – so try several rehearsals before you dub the camera-clicking sound on to the tape.

Now, on to the reception. Your next question must be, do I record all the speeches? That really depends on their quality as much as anything else, and one of the most useful pieces of research you could carry out beforehand is to listen to each of the speechmakers rehearsing their words, and jokes, beforehand. This will help you make your decisions, and might provide some good footage, especially if some of the other members of the family sit in, so that you can record their reactions, and follow the way in which the speaker changes and improves his speech as a result. If you pick out the highlights of two or three of the scripts at this stage, whether or not you include them in the preparations section of the programme, and if you take notes of the contents of each space, you should then know roughly when the highlights you shot being rehearsed are due to come up. All you need to do is shoot the start of each speech, cut away to some of the watching faces, and fade the sound down to a lower level, before cutting back to the speaker just before the highlight and lifting the sound again.

Once the excerpt has passed, you can cut away again, fading the sound and going into 'pause' mode, until you know the speech is coming to an end – cut back to the speaker one last time, and fade up the sound, so that you can capture the end of the speech, and the resulting toast. Do that for each of the main speakers, and you've covered the reception. But how do you end it – on a pile of empty champagne bottles, on the bride's father leafing through a pile of bills with an expression of consternation on his face, on the couple's car trailing tins and old boots away down the road? That's up to you. . . .

IN FRONT OF THE CAMERA

Chapter 13

So far we have concentrated on the art of programme-making from behind the camera – in the role of producer, director, camera operator, and editor. Now we're going to take a look at the action on the other end of the lens – either to act as presenter, or how to direct other people in setting up commentaries or interviews to make your programmes more varied.

If you look at several television documentaries on a wide variety of subjects, you will find that some will limit commentary to a disembodied voice-over, telling the story through pictures of subjects which don't communicate with the audience directly. Others rely on a presenter to explain, to amplify, to underline, and generally carry through a closer relationship between the programme and its audience. And programmes of both types often include interviews with people who have a contribution to make to the subject – from one-line quotes, through to longer and more formal interviews which may sometimes make up complete programmes in themselves.

The first thing to understand about working in front of the camera is that there's no mystique about it. All kinds of people find they have a natural gift for communication through the television screen, and even those who don't possess this inborn ability can still learn how to appear relaxed and convincing on screen. Many companies exist purely to train actors, politicians, and company executives how to 'come over' well on television, so highly prized is this skill of talking to the camera. And in taking your first steps as an on-screen performer, you have one powerful advantage over all these other people: you can arrange things so that you can try out your first practice sessions with no-one else watching. Not for you the intimidating presence of a full television crew, the lights, and the complex signals between the director and the floor manager. You can practice in your own time, and in complete privacy, and you may well end up being surprised by how easy it is.

Let's begin by deciding where to practice talking to the camera. You've two main alternatives: indoors or outdoors. The advantage of indoors as a location means you have no travelling to do. You can set up a 'news-studio' type background at home with a desk and a couple of lights, and you can work in complete privacy. The disadvantages are that unless you're careful with the lights, you may be so taken aback by the way your face appears in close-up, with shadows and hollows emphasised more than they would be with a more carefully prepared lighting combination, that you won't assess your own performance with the objectivity it deserves.

An outdoor location in broad daylight avoids this problem. Another advantage is that, if the background is unusual or unexpected, it can provide you with a natural subject for conversation with the camera – but more of that in a moment. Do you need an assistant, to operate the camera? It makes life easier, in the sense that you have less to concentrate on, but if you feel happiest taking the first lesson on your own, there's no reason why you shouldn't mount the camera on a tripod and do the entire job yourself.

Let's assume that the first practice session is a solo one. Find yourself a location where you won't be disturbed, where the view provides a suitable backdrop to whatever you're going to say, and where there won't be problems of noise, or traffic or anything else to act as a distraction. First of all, decide where you're going to stand to deliver your piece to camera – not with the sun behind you, or you'll disappear into a dramatic silhouette outlined against the glare. Mark the spot with an empty tape box, then move back to the camera and set up the shot as if you were shooting an imaginary person on that spot – which in a sense you are. It's a good idea to begin with an empty tape, since these first trials will be untidy and a certain amount of waste is inevitable.

Set the camera to begin recording, and walk back to your mark and look into the camera lens, counting from one to ten slowly. Then walk back to the camera, wind the tape back to the beginning, and replay what you've just recorded. What we are looking for now is your positioning – nothing more. Are you in the centre of the screen? Does the camera need to be tilted down or up to produce the shot you need – do you need to zoom in or out, or do you, as presenter, need to move your position to left or right? Make whatever corrections you think are needed, set the camera to record again, walk back to your mark, look into the lens, and count to ten all over again. Then walk back, rewind the tape, and check the results. Keep on doing this until you're satisfied that the shot, and your positioning, at least are right.

Now it's time for you to talk to the camera. On the face of it, there's something slightly ridiculous about ignoring all the people on a crowded set and talking directly to an inanimate and unresponsive object like a camera lens. Since you're on your own anyway, this shouldn't be so much of a problem in this case – but it DOES demand a genuine effort of imagination. Try thinking of the camera as an old friend whom you know well, but a friend to whom you want to tell something, either a story they won't have heard, or an issue which is going to affect them directly, or a subject they're going to find interesting. You need to speak clearly, you need to look at them while you're speaking to them, but otherwise you need to be as natural and as unaffected as you would be if you were talking to a genuine friend.

But what are you going to say? All of us have dozens of conversations with all kinds of people every day, without ever having to prepare what we're going to say in any detail. But talking to a camera, or for that matter a tape recorder, even on a one-to-one basis, has an inhibiting effect. Because what we say is going to be preserved, we don't want to make any mistakes, we don't want to stumble over words, and we don't want to dry up and forget what we were going to say next. All these are very human reactions, and everyone has much the same feelings when going before a camera for the first time. But remember your advantage: the tape can easily be erased, and no-one is going to see the results of these practice sessions unless you want them to. So forget about the need to produce a polished performance right from the beginning. Let's concentrate instead on finding something to say which will at least give you one less problem to worry about.

Some people think the right way to speak to camera is like the right way they would approach making a speech. They would spend a lot of time writing it, polishing it and improving it until it was just about perfect, and then they'd commit it to memory, learning it until they could reproduce it effortlessly from beginning to end. But there are two drawbacks to this approach. One is that it takes far too long, and more importantly, it will come over very badly indeed. You may remember all the words from start to finish, but unless you're a talented actor to begin with, they won't sound either sincere or spontaneous: we make up ordinary conversations as we go along, and this is the effect to strive for.

A prepared speech sounds contrived and stilted by comparison, even if you don't dry up halfway: when repeating something parrot-fashion, even when it's something you've written yourself, the danger is that your attention can wander. You can suddenly start thinking about the situation you're in, and then your memory can start playing tricks – without thinking about your words and what you want to say, you forget. You can't remember what comes next, and without a prompter, you're lost. So leave learning one's lines to the actors; that's what they're trained to do. A good actor can read a page from the telephone directory and make it sound interesting – but most of us can only do that with material WE find interesting. Which means something new, something fresh, above all something WE feel strongly about.

Let's try an example of that. It's worth bringing along a book, or better still a newspaper, and try using that as a script. Set the camera running, walk to your mark and then read out an item to camera, looking up and starting the camera firmly in the lens every so often. Then stop, go back to the camera, wind the tape back and play back the result. You'll probably find that having something to concentrate on – reading the news item to camera – gave you the chance to turn in a surprisingly unruffled performance. But look at the way in which you related to the camera. When you looked into the lens, did you look like someone scanning an inanimate object in a museum, or reacting to a person you didn't know, or didn't want to know? Or were you friendly, informative, relaxed? Looking at yourself as objectively as an ordinary member of the audience, were you convinced by what you, as the presenter or newsreader, were actually saying?

Try this routine several times, so that you become more relaxed with the camera, and try reacting to the subject matter. If the subject is an amusing one, try a smile. If it's an amazing or unlikely one, try thinking yourself into the kind of expressions and gestures you would use in telling this to a friend – perhaps reading them a piece aloud from a newspaper in the pub, in the train, or in the living room at home. In time, you'll find your performance is less wooden, more relaxed, more human, and more convincing.

Now it's time to try something a little more ambitious. The only problem with reading a piece aloud from a book or a newspaper is that an image of someone reading is a pretty boring picture, however interesting the text they're reading. The only time they relate to the camera is when they look up, straight into the lens. So practise memorising a line or two at a time, so that you can extend the periods of eye contact, and react more convincingly to what you're actually saying, before looking down again in time to find your place and carry on with the reading. When you've become accustomed to that, and made a note of the effect that greater eye contact, and more obvious emphasis of the key words in the piece can bring to your delivery, try using the printed text as a prop. Read from it, and then start a conversation based on it. If it's an item about something silly or provocative, take that as your starting point, and tell your friend (the camera lens) what YOU think about what you've just been reading. Try this several times, until your conversation becomes more relaxed and more spontaneous.

Now let's try a completely unrehearsed talk to the camera. Try to think of a subject about which you feel strongly – either something about which you're very fond or, probably better, some news item or some trend or some aspect of human behaviour which makes you very worried or very angry. Think for a moment or two – no more, as too much thought can be inhibiting, as it gives you too much which you feel you HAVE to remember – and launch into your piece. Don't worry about having to pause now and again. If your piece is genuinely spontaneous, which this is, then these pauses will emphasise that you're thinking for yourself, and not working from a script. Try the same technique with different subjects. Talk about a family occasion, or what happened at work yesterday, or a film, or a television programme you've seen recently. Anything in fact, which doesn't mean you making something up in advance – any subject which will allow you to talk off the cuff, without having a prepared script, or without having to search around for what to say next.

When you've practised with several different subjects, try playing back the whole tape from start to finish. You should find that your improvement in relaxation and confidence in front of the camera is clear and obvious, and that it's now a much less daunting prospect than it was before. You will also find that spontaneous pieces delivered directly to camera are more interesting to watch, and more convincing to listen to, than pieces which you're reading to camera, with more intermittent eye contact between you and the camera lens.

The next step is to take a helper on location with you – at the very least, someone who can operate the camera to your instructions in some more ambitious presenter routines. The ideal would be another home-video enthusiast, so that you can try out different ideas and approaches from both points of view: from behind the camera, as well as in front of it.

For example, one useful device for bringing a presenter into the picture smoothly and effortlessly is to pan from a shot of the subject to reveal the presenter standing nearby. As the camera turns and reveals the presenter, he or she turns smoothly to camera and speaks. At the end of the piece, the picture either cuts to something else entirely, or the camera might pan back to the original start of the shot, leaving the presenter out of frame after his or her final words. This means the presenter needs to know something from the camera operator – when he's in shot and it's time for the piece to camera to begin. And the camera operator needs to know something from the presenter – some word or phrase or line which will tell the camera operator that the presenter's piece is finishing, so the camera operator can be ready for the cut, or the pan away to the closing frame of the shot.

In practice, the signal for the presenter to begin his or her piece – the presenter's cue – can be given in several ways. A shout of 'action', a wave from someone out of frame, but within the presenter's eye line, even a nod from the camera operator. What it means from the presenter's point of view is being able to launch into a piece, no matter how spontaneous, at the given signal, whatever form that signal might take. It takes practice – so practice it, with as many different subjects, and types of cue as possible.

After the first couple of attempts, try and decide what your end words should be. Agree these with your camera operator, and then practise ending with the vital phrase, however varied and spontaneous your words may have been along the way. And another useful skill is being able to time your piece, however roughly. Try to speak for about a minute on your chosen subject. Play it back, timing it with a stopwatch, and see how accurate your estimate was. Then try again, and see if you can improve your accuracy, before trying to speak for two minutes, or for thirty seconds at a time.

There are two good reasons for learning how to present material effectively to camera. One of them is to master the skills yourself, to improve the standard of your own video productions. The other is to be able to persuade others to appear in front of the camera. By being able to show them how it should be done, you can indirectly reassure them there's nothing intimidating about speaking to camera, and you can advise them from your own experience on how to correct and improve the impression they make on the screen.

Now let's change places again: back to our original position, behind the camera. We'll assume that after practising the art of presenting to camera, you've found a friend, a relative, or a colleague who is able and willing to stand in for you as a presenter in your productions.

How and when can you use them to best advantage in a programme? The answer will depend very much on the type of programme, and on the actual subject matter, and some of these examples are discussed in more detail. But as a more general principle, you can use a presenter to bring a more personal perspective to a subject, to explain and emphasise those parts of the subject which may be difficult to cover otherwise in pictures.

For example, in covering a current issue of some kind, like a controversial road scheme or a public enquiry, a presenter can bring us up-to-date on what's happened so far: a historical perspective which may be difficult to create in any other way. And we've all seen television programmes where companies and institutions have refused to comment on what's been said. A good way to tell the audience about that refusal is to stand a presenter outside the headquarters of the body involved and explain what they were asked to do, and the words in which they announced their refusal.

There are probably hundreds of other ways in which a presenter can be used to make a subject more immediate and more intelligible to the audience. Presenters are useful for making explanations comprehensible. They can use gestures, or even simple props, to explain the principles behind something which may otherwise be very difficult to deduce from the pictures. A good presenter can interview contributors and generally anchor the programme together – and when you have a positive point or opinion to put over, seeing a presenter deliver it can be more convincing than the same words, delivered by a disembodied voice-over.

But how can we use a presenter visually? A series of cuts to and from a subject to a presenter, then back to the subject, back to the presenter, and so on, would be counter-productive, apart from being boring, as they would hint at a separation between subject and presenter which would work against the impression you're trying to create.

So try to think of ways in which you can make the presenter part of the action. Always try to compose the picture with the presenter in front of a background which is very much part of the subject you're looking at. If you're making a programme on a race-meeting, either place your presenter in the paddock, or in the stand, or in the car park, or even in the road outside, as long as what appears behind him or her in the picture says 'race-meeting'. And experiment with pans to and from your presenter, with change-focus shots to move directly from subject to presenter and vice-versa, where the geometry of the subject and the surroundings allow, and even with having your presenter walk out from the subject-matter itself.

If you're shooting a boat, having the presenter climb out of a hatchway and walk to the edge of the deck, before delivering his or her piece to camera, would be an effective entrance to make. To return to our train departure example in an earlier chapter, the presenter could make a piece to camera by appearing at a corridor window of the leading coach when the train is about to leave. By cutting from the end of the presenter's piece to a shot of the guard blowing his whistle, and then a shot of the train pulling out, you have a very powerful exit sequence to round off the story perfectly.

One point more, before we leave the business of speaking directly to camera. We've tended to concentrate on the idea of knowing what you want to say, and saying it as fluently and as convincingly as you can, to produce the kind of presentation which is needed. There are other ways of remembering what needs to be said which are used by professional presenters – who are very often speaking to a script written by someone else in any case. One is the autocue: a printed script which is scrolled upwards over a special screen reflected in a pane of glass held at an angle to the camera lens. The camera sees the presenter clearly through the glass – but the presenter sees the reflection of the script, and can read it directly while looking straight into the lens.

The other method, which some – but by no means all – presenters are able to use is to record themselves delivering the piece on to a miniature audio recorder, like a Walkman. They then place the recorder in a pocket, and play back the recording into a small earpiece which can't be seen by the camera. When they deliver their piece to camera, they're repeating what their own recorded voice is saying into their own ear, but a fraction of a second later. It takes an accurate sense of timing and a lot of concentration, but anyone who can master the technique can find it a powerful aid to recording a long and complicated piece of script. But like anything else which isn't being said in your own words, and from your own thoughts, it does demand the extra skill of injecting the right amount of emphasis and animation to make it sound spontaneous and convincing.

Now we'll move to the other way of involving people in the programme: interviewing, and recording quotes from contributors. Many of the requirements are the same for interviewees as they are for presenters. Their words need to sound genuinely their own, and the more spontaneous and convincing their delivery, the better. But there are two important differences. They're being prompted, to an important extent, by the presenter or interviewer asking them questions, and reacting to their answers, which does help keep things moving. And today's television style means that they aren't usually shot looking and speaking directly into the camera lens, but looking off-camera in the direction of the interviewer. Even if we never see or hear a question being asked, the quote or statement from the contributor will still be delivered as if he's speaking to someone present with the camera, rather than to the camera itself.

This last fact makes things easier in two ways. For one thing, it's less intimidating and more natural to speak to a person rather than the lens of the camera. Second, because the contributor isn't trying to stare directly into the lens, it is possible to use 'idiot cards' to prompt his memory in areas where statistics or other complex facts are needed as part of the answer.

All this means is a set of cards with the salient facts or figures written in large print on them, can be held up in front of the interviewer's face at the appropriate point in the interview. The print needs to be large as even a short-sighted contributor mustn't be seen to peer or squint at the cards – nothing would reveal he's reading from prepared material more clearly. Because the cards are held up in front of the interviewer's face – who is out of shot anyway – the contributor doesn't have to change his eye-line to read them. And if the cards are limited to the barest essentials, there isn't the temptation for him to read his script, and seem more wooden and unconvincing as a result. So stick to those points which are difficult to remember – figures, dates, percentages, proper names, unfamiliar words and anything else where absolute precision is important. Otherwise, keep props like these to the minimum.

Now to shooting an interview itself. Let's assume that you've decided in planning what a particular contributor has to say, on a list of four questions which the presenter should put to him. Assuming that the interview will start with a piece by the presenter to introduce the interview, followed by a turn to the contributor, or even a straight cut to the two of them for the first time, the initial shot would show both the interviewer and the person being interviewed. But once the contributor starts answering the question, you can start zooming in to hold them in close-up for most of the answer. If it's simply a quote, rather than a formal interview, then the recording starts with their answer, framed in close-up anyway.

If the contributor, and the interviewer are happy to continue, stay in close-up for the whole of the answer to the question. In fact, a professional crew shooting an interview would probably shoot the whole interview, however many questions were involved, as a close-up on the contributor. Then they would change the camera position to shoot each of the interviewer's questions in close-up, so that these can be edited into the finished sequence at the appropriate times. Without that kind of editing capability, though, you'd have to shoot an interview question by question and answer by answer.

But what happens if the interviewee makes a mistake, or dries up in the middle of an answer? Brief them beforehand, that if they hit either of these problems, to 'freeze'. In other words, they should simply stop and remain looking at the questioner, without saying anything more, or shaking their head, or looking at the camera, or whatever – this makes it easier to edit the next section of the interview after the pause. Then, when they're ready to carry on talking again, you can press the 'start' button and resume recording – provided you have some way of bridging the slight jump-cut which would otherwise result.

There are two ways of doing this. If your camera is limited to assemble editing, then you need to move it to shoot the questioner, as if you were going to record a question. This means setting up the camera so that the questioner is looking past the camera in the opposite direction to the contributor. For example, if the contributor is slightly to the right of the screen, looking towards the left-hand edge of the screen (to give him 'talking room'), then you need to pose the questioner on the left-hand side of the screen, looking to the right of the camera, for the geometry of the shot to work.

Once you're in the right place on the tape, and ready to record, ask your questioner to look as if he's listening to, and agreeing with, what the contributor has just been saying. Because these reaction shots tend to involve a nod of the head, they're known in television as 'noddies', and they're usually shot once the interview is over. But the purpose is the same. If an answer to a question has to be shot in several sections, a cut to one of the questioner's 'noddies' provides an instant cutaway to bridge the jump-cuts which would result from editing the different pieces of the answer together.

All you need is a very brief shot of the questioner, before returning to the contributor for him to finish an answer. But don't forget that you don't have to use everything which has been recorded so far. If you feel the best of the answer was at the beginning, and the contributor has fallen for the common fault of repeating himself towards the end, all you need do is play the whole of his response back to find a natural pause, make a note of the words leading up to that pause, and agree with your contributor what the next words should be to lead smoothly into the concluding part of his answer. Once you've set up the edit at the right spot, recorded the 'noddy' and then set up the camera in the original position, give your contributor the cue, and off you go with the rest of his answer. If it doesn't work first time, wind the tape back to the 'noddy' and record it again as a second take – and keep on doing it until you record a take which works properly.

If, however, your camera is fitted with an 'insert edit' capability, you don't have to pause to shoot each 'noddy' needed to cover any pause or gap in the contributor's answers. You can edit the whole answer together, then move the camera and set up to shoot the questioner, after which you can shoot as many 'noddies' as you need to cover all the gaps where the answer has been edited together. Because the insert edit leaves the original sound-track running throughout, only placing the new picture over the old as an overlay, it's ideal for this kind of work. But it does mean you can't shoot the questions afterwards, since you do need to hear the questioner asking them as well as see him on screen – so these have to be shot in order once the previous answer has been completed. Finally, don't forget that even if your contributor is word-perfect, you can, and should be prepared to use 'noddies' as visual relief. Of course, if you are able to edit the finished programme together on your VCR, you can go back and shoot the presenter asking all his questions in order, and simply edit these into the interview before the appropriate answer in each case.

There's also another kind of cutaway which you can use to vary the picture in a long or complicated interview: if the interview is taking place in a location where the background actually relates to what is being said. To take an earlier example, if the sequence shot on the preserved railway was to include an interview with the driver of the engine about what driving a steam locomotive really involves, then be on the lookout for cutaways to match what he's actually saying. For example, if he refers to the need to keep oiling the valve gear, then you can shoot him afterwards going round the engine with the oilcan – but record it as an insert edit over him saying that part of his answer. If he talks about the safety valves on the boiler, shoot them as an insert edit over that part of the interview, and so on. Every cutaway shot you can find will add to the variety and interest of the interview.

One final word on interviews. Sometimes a programme calls for a series of quotes from different people, rather than a longer interview with one or two contributors. If you're trying to canvass reactions from a wide group – like passers-by on a local redevelopment scheme – these are often referred to as 'vox-pop' interviews, the term being Latin for 'voice of the people'. All you need do is record the original question you're going to put to each of your contributors, once only. Let's assume that in this case, it's 'What do YOU think of the new shopping development?' You either record your interviewer saying, to camera, something like 'We asked local people what THEY thought of the new shopping development', or you record a shot of the development itself, or the site, if we're talking about some plan for the future, with a voice-over commentary (see Chapter Nine) asking a different version of the question to explain who the contributors are – like 'What do local shoppers think of the proposed shopping development?'

Once the introduction has been shot, in whatever form you see it, you're then free to shoot as many vox-pop responses to that question as you want. But it makes for more picture variety if you shoot them alternately to left of frame and to right of frame. You can also vary the background, if time and space allow, but it's more important that they face in alternate directions, since they're the main focus of interest in each case. If you CAN see much of the background behind them, try to make sure it's clearly part of the place we've just been looking at, as a reminder that the interviews were conducted on the spot, and didn't relate to some other location altogether.

The routine is much the same in each case. Place your subject in front of the right background, and looking to whichever side of the camera is appropriate. Explain to them the question you're going to ask, and the fact that you want a short, simple answer – something preferably longer than a 'yes' or a 'no', but not a long and rambling paragraph saying the same thing at much greater length. Frame the picture as you want it, moving the contributor to left or right to avoid placing them against trees or telephone poles, then set the camera up in the 'pause' mode. Give them a rehearsal if it makes them feel less nervous. Some professional cameramen and directors offer a dry run to nervous contributors and then shoot it anyway, since they're likely to be much less nervous if they think the camera isn't turning. Then ask them the question, press the start button, and off you go.

There's no need for shots of the interviewer, or of any 'noddies', in this kind of mass interview. If you want to ask other questions, then bring the interviewer in to ask them to camera, or in voice-over, and then follow the question with a set of replies. But if anyone doesn't work as a contributor, either on a single take, or throughout, then treat it as a mistake. Go back on the tape to the end of the previous contribution, and start again with another take. Sometimes people will become less nervous with repetition, but sometimes their nervousness will increase, to the point where there's no purpose in continuing, and you'd be well advised to thank them politely and move on to the next contributor. If you do, don't forget to record the new contribution over the last take of the previous one, and record them in the same position, otherwise your alternate left-right framing sequence will be disturbed.

Two more points which are worth making about interviews, or indeed any contributions from the public in programmes both professional and amateur. These kinds of pictures are called 'talking heads', and it can be wise to be careful about how much of them you use. It all depends on how interesting they are. Sometimes people have so interesting a story to tell that you could have a half-hour programme of nothing but someone's reminiscences; but that kind of quality is rare. Sometimes you may have a succession of vox-pop interviews, candid expressions of what real people (rather than people working to a script) feel about the subject. Sometimes their interest is in the fact that the feelings they portray are unanimous although their diversity is what makes them worth recording. As always, be on the lookout for how your audience is likely to feel – and if you feel the talking heads are taking over the programme then cut them down, or alternatively, look for cutaways and overlay shots of whatever it is they're actually talking about.

The second option, if you want to include people talking, but want to turn to a different image on screen, yet you don't have any chance to shoot the subject matter of their talk – is to shoot the contributors doing something else, which is characteristic of them. If a man is talking to you about the changes in the town since his childhood, you can always include a long cutaway of him fishing, walking through the town centre, or simply sitting and looking at the river. Try to pick something which has a relationship, however distant, with what he's talking about, and something with plenty of colour and variety, which will allow you to go on shooting from different angles and viewpoints to cover the longest possible interview you might want to record with him. Once again, this is a lot more straightforward if you are able to edit the cutaways into the finished programme where they are needed — in that case, you can even go and shoot them at different locations or on different occasions if need be, before editing them into the finished programme at the right place.

DRAMA

We're now going to turn our attention to the drama production where the location, the characters, the storyline and the dialogue are created from your imagination. It might be anything from a stage classic performed by members of the local amateur dramatic society or a one-act story, performed by friends and family. Either way, the objectives, and the problems, of producing a gripping and convincing result on the screen will be the same – and they'll have much in common with the priorities faced by those producing broadcast drama with a six-figure budget.

Because the range of subjects and abilities is so very wide, we will have to begin by making one or two assumptions. We'll take it that your cast is small, that we're considering a single set, and the storyline is a fairly simple one – no point, after all, in trying to run before you can walk. On the other hand, if we assume that your cast have no acting experience at all, then the amount of coaching and teaching you would have to do would fill a book like this one, and leave no room for anything else. We'll also assume that the set is built and dressed (that is, furnished with the props and furniture which make it look convincing, in the context of the play) and that it's been lit so that you can shoot the opening part of the scene. All the cast know their lines, and what you have to do is turn that stage ability into a production which works well on the screen.

In one respect, shooting a scripted drama is easier for you, as producer or director. The script tells you who speaks next, and what they're going to say. All you have to consider is how the lines should be said – laying the stress on different words in a simple sentence can alter its meaning quite radically creating all kinds of implications. One famous murder case hinged on what was meant by a criminal facing arrest saying to his accomplice, who had a gun, 'Let him have it'. Did he mean that the other man should hand over the gun, as the policeman had asked, several times? Or did he mean that he should shoot the policeman? In the end, the other man took the second meaning, as did the jury – the policeman was killed, and the man who shouted the words was hanged as an accessory to the murder. So pay attention to how each piece of dialogue is actually said. Make sure that the emphasis and the rhythm help the actors to create the meaning you want them to deliver in each of the lines.

If you're working with actors – even amateur actors – who are used to stage acting rather than film or television acting, then you may have to advise them on gestures. In the smaller confines of the television screen, the audience has a much closer view, and movements and patterns of speech which would seem subtle in the theatre would appear as grossly exaggerated. Run a few test shots of each one speaking and acting a few lines, and show them how every change in facial expression, every flicker of the eyes, is picked up with total clarity in close-up.

These points can be checked and refined in rehearsals. The other purpose of rehearsing is for you to write your camera script – to tell yourself what shots you need to capture the whole of the dramatic action. If you have three actors on stage, it would be boring to stay in wide-shot to capture all three all the time. You may need a close-up of whoever is speaking or a two-shot, to capture both the speaker and the reaction of the others at once. Keep a variety of shots, while always being aware of the need to show the audience the drama within the play.

One of the problems of shooting a play for film or video is that you have to break it up into individual shots. Only then can you move the camera or reframe the picture for the next shot. Some actors may find it difficult to pick up the rhythm of their performance, and you might find it worth letting them have a run-up to each shot. If they act out the minute or so of dialogue and movement which leads up to the shot, it will give you a perfect cue when to start recording.

If you have a full edit capability between your camera and your VCR, then you can treat each scene as a whole. Shoot it from start to finish concentrating on showing the scene as a whole – then shoot it again, this time concentrating on one of the main characters. If you repeat this for each of the others on stage (unless it is a crowd scene, when you will have to concentrate on the three or four most important people on stage), then you have the option of editing the final version together in whatever way will best suit the action of the drama.

Finally, always listen to what your actors have to say about the parts they are playing, the gestures, movements and emphases they make. Very often a movement, which may not be in the script, might add a great deal to our insight into a character. The way your cast stand, sit, and move all contribute to the characters they're trying to portray – but in the end, it's you – the producer – who has to balance all these factors together to produce a coherent whole. You have to see the play from the audience's point of view, and if you can enjoy it and follow it, then you're more than halfway home.

THE PROFESSIONALS – EQUIPMENT

Chapter 15

Through the course of the book, we have been examining ways of bringing a home produced video closer to the kind of professional results we can all see every night on our television screens at home. The message which should have emerged very clearly is that an awful lot can be done through attitudes and ideas, careful planning and an eye for opportunity, to achieve good results with a minimum of equipment and the lowest possible cost. But where there is a difference, given the cost of specialist video equipment, between the talented amateur and the run-of-the-mill professional, it must be in the sophistication and the capabilities of the equipment each one is able to use.

In recent years, however, two things have happened to narrow that gap. The first trend is for home video equipment to offer a great deal more in the way of sophisticated features for a reasonable price. Insert editing, character generators, and automatic white balance were all restricted to professional equipment only a short while ago. In the next few years, other features will be added to narrow the gap still further, so fast is the pace of development and so keen the spur of competition. But in the meantime, there's a second factor at work. Anyone who has a particularly ambitious production in mind, or the backing of a generous budget, can hire virtually any item of equipment that's needed, with or without an experienced operator as well.

In the case of the camera, perhaps the greatest differences are not in what the professional camera can do which the amateur's camera can not – rather more in the way in which it can do it, and the range of those abilities. Today's professional cameras can cope better with constrasts, since the increasing use of CCD arrays rather than tubes mean that internal circuitry in the camera can tone down the signals it picks up from an over-bright sky, and amplify the signals from a backlit subject, so that shots which would be lost with your camera might at least become possible. In the same way, the picture can be lifted when you're shooting in low light levels – each time you have to amplify the picture signal, you're having to amplify the background noise as well, so the picture becomes less sharp and more grainy as you lift the amplication factor. But you DO get a picture, in light which might previously have given you little better than a confusion of shifting silhouettes and shadows.

Tripods and camera mounts are more sophisticated too. Genuine, fluid-head tripods are designed to make complicated tilting and panning shots much easier to do smoothly. They can lift the camera high up for elevated shots, or shorter legs can allow low-level shots. Wheeled dollies for tracking shots and hydraulically operated arms can provide smooth movements over several feet or even high into the air. If necessary to provide smooth movement over rough ground for a tracking shot or a walking interview, you can hire bolt-together rails along which a special camera dolly can be made to run.

Camera lenses will work in the same way as the lens on your camera – but zooms will be much longer. Ratios of ten to one or fourteen or more to one are common on professional equipment, rather than the four or six to one ratios of most home-video cameras. You may still have the recorder fitted as part of the camera – this is becoming more common on professional outfits for ease of handling and speed of movement. Miniature recorders usually work on MII Betacam or Betacam SP – essentially a VHS or Betamax cassette running at much higher speed to record all the extra data needed for a broadcast-quality picture.

Other recorders are used as separate units, linked by cable to the camera, and a professional crew working on location will usually take a portable colour monitor as well, to give you more information than a playback through the black-and-white viewfinder will give you. Another advantage, when you're directing, is that you can see the shot as the cameraman is recording it, and you will know whether another take is necessary or not.

But the biggest difference between a professional shoot, whatever type of equipment they use, and your own is the luxury of not having to edit within the camera. Sometimes you may not be able to decide between two different ways of shooting a particular shot – does it work better in medium-shot or in close-up? When you're able to edit the programme back at base, you can hedge your bets and shoot both, taking the final decision when you see the whole edited sequence. Or your presenter may make a mistake in each take of a long and complicated piece – you might be able to edit together a good first half and a good second half of a different take to make an acceptable result.

You can also shoot more efficiently, since you don't have to shoot in strict picture order. You can shoot all the sequences relating to one part of the location, before moving to the next part, and so on – a real blessing, with heavy equipment to move, and perhaps a need to relight after the move. And you can shoot cutaways and details afterwards, for editing into the programme later.

Finally, small items of extra equipment can be hired to make your job easier. If you have to cue someone over a long distance, like someone who has to drive a car into shot around a far-off bend in the road, you can talk to them over a set of two-way radios. This allows you to know exactly when they're coming, for running up the camera and recorder, and you can also relay last-minute changes of plan and detailed instructions to them.

But the biggest change of all is in the post-production phase of making the programme: editing the finished result together from the shots you've recorded on location. Even if the results are being edited together on a VHS or S-VHS edit suite, the flexibility it provides can transform your programme beyond recognition.

An edit suite works by copying extracts from the tape recorded by your camera (or from any other source), which are then played back over an input, or player machine and copied on to the finished programme tape which is being recorded on a second machine. Because you can specify, to the individual frame, where each shot starts and finishes, and where the edit is to be performed on the programme tape, the edit suite allows you to time cuts and changes to perfection. You can also choose whether to edit just pictures, leaving the sound track intact, or whether to edit one or other of the two sound channels, leaving the pictures alone, or whether to edit in any combination of these.

This flexibility allows you to build up a sound track from pre-recorded commentary, sound effects tapes, the sound already recorded on location, or added background music, and all the time the sound is being edited exactly where you want it in relation to the pictures. Finally, the edit suite will perform any edit you select as a preview, so you can watch it on the monitor as a rehearsal. Only when you're completely satisfied need you press the 'edit' button to perform the edit in reality.

The simple two-machine edit suite is a wonderfully versatile piece of equipment, and well worth the usual rate for hiring it, in terms of what it can achieve. But it can't perform mixes between one picture sequence and another, and it can't superimpose titles, graphics, and other special effects. To perform mixes, you need to hire a three-machine edit suite, which is usually more expensive. The tape containing the sequences from which you're mixing is placed in one of the player machines, with the tape containing the sequence you're mixing TO placed in the second player, and the master programme tape in the recorder. All you then have to decide is where the sequence from each of the source tapes begins and ends, how long the mix lasts, and where it begins on the programme tape, and the machinery does the rest, as a preview or as an edit.

Special effects generators can add a great deal more, to either a two-machine or three-machine edit. You can either type in titles or captions, and then superimpose them on your recorded sequences wherever you like, but you can also specify the colours and sizes of the letters too. You can superimpose one picture on another, use one picture to wipe the other off the screen, or appear through the first picture in a variety of complicated patterns. Computer-graphics generators are more expensive but even more versatile. A good first step is a visit to a specialized facilities house, to see what these different pieces of equipment can do, so that you can decide when one is worthwhile, or even essential, to a production which you have in mind.

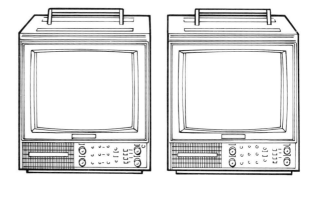

In a professional editing suite each VCR has its own monitor. At least one will be a high-quality colour set (*above*). As the name implies, the monitor's role is to allow the editor to keep track of transmissions from a VCR or from a video camera. The edit control unit (*below*) enables the editor to preview edits, program sequences into its memory for automatic editing, return the tape automatically to pre-set positions and keep a frame-accurate tally of its progress. It has a set of controls for both VCRs.

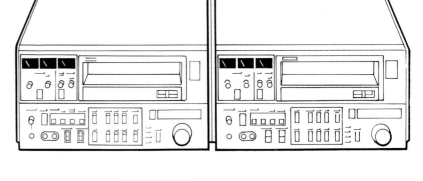

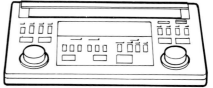

THE PROFESSIONALS – PRODUCTION

Chapter 16

Seeing a professional television production in the making may be a bewildering experience. Most studio productions use several different cameras at once, with the producer, director, and vision mixer switching from one to another, as the next cameraman is being cued to frame his next shot. This means the whole programme may be shot as a live production from start to finish even if, as is more likely, it's being recorded on tape for transmission, or re-transmission on a later occasion. Because of this, it may need the minimum of editing: but it takes a lot of rehearsal, and a whole squad of specialists on the studio floor to back up the camera operators and sound recordists – lighting, make-up, floor managers, set designers, and a whole team of video and audio engineers monitoring the quality of the material being recorded.

In fact, the studio recording is probably the result of many months of preparation, particularly if a historical drama production is being put together. This is the most expensive kind of programme to make, in costs per hour of finished material, since the combination of having to use professional actors and carefully chosen locations in addition to studio sets and costumes which have to be accurate to the smallest period detail, is enormously expensive. Specialists will have had to advise on props and interiors. What kind of wine-glasses would look right in a small country house in the middle of the eighteenth century, and what kind of colours would have been in fashion for the interior decoration? Similarly, fashions in clothes and hairstyles have to be researched and re-created to be as correct as possible – and the lighting has to be capable of striking a balance between the needs of the equipment and making the resulting picture look as though the room was lit by oil-lamps, gaslight or even flickering torches or rushlights.

Other studio productions are inherently much cheaper and easier to stage. Panel games and quiz shows are recorded in little longer than the length of each programme, and they're often recorded in batches, with several weeks' programmes being recorded in a single day to economise on sets, lighting, personnel and travelling for the contestants. For all that, the process is a complicated one, with the action being shared between several cameras and the sound being picked up by a whole array of microphones. The careful mixing which produces the pictures and sound which is recorded for the audience to see is done in the control rooms while the show progresses, with the minimum of interruptions for corrections to be made or faults to be rectified.

The other main type of programme would be much more familiar territory – the single camera documentary. Here the production process would be much the same as the examples we've been outlining through the course of the book, except that the crew would be larger, the equipment heavier and more complex, and, of course, the editing would be done afterwards, on a full edit suite.

It's equally true that not all location shoots may involve one single camera. Outside broadcasts of major events ranging from a Cup Final to a Royal wedding can be far more complex than any studio production. Either signals will be relayed back to mixing consoles and control rooms back in the main studios, so that the outside-broadcast crews are working as they would in a studio production, but at a much longer reach, or the control rooms are on location, in specially-fitted equipment vans. And the programme will be made up as it's shot, and may even be transmitted live as well as being recorded, so that the highlights of the ceremony or the event can be edited later – in all these respects, the techniques, the team and the equipment are much closer to studio productions than they are to genuine location shooting.

To confuse the picture still further, there are times when location shooting can involve more than one camera, too. If part of what they're shooting is by nature unrepeatable, like the launching of a ship or the take-off of an aircraft, there may be a sound argument for shooting it through two, three or even more cameras, to have several different perspectives on it for editing afterwards. But the crucial difference is that, even with more than a single camera, the shots are all brought back for editing afterwards.

Apart from this extra flexibility which editing allows, most of the actual shooting would seem remarkably similar to the techniques we've been discussing in this book. Shots need to be set up, and timed, and rehearsed. Performers need to be coached and cued, and takes need to be repeated until they are right. Scenes need to be lit, though the lighting crew and the batteries of lights and the generators and long cables may seem a lavish accessory, they can work surprisingly quickly when the rest of the production is waiting for a new lighting setup.

There are riggers and engineers to set up the specialist camera mounts, from railway tracks to scaffolding towers, and then there's all the other ways of transporting a camera, and the operator, to where they can do their job. Cameras can be carried on cars – mounted on a specially strengthened flat roof or shooting through an opened window, depending on the viewpoint that's wanted. They can be carried aloft in aeroplanes or in helicopters, where vibration can become a problem – so they're often carried on a gyro-stabilised mounting, which damps out anything from a steady vibration to any sudden swerves or lurches. Some of them are so effective that a cameraman can even run down a flight of steps in a chase sequence, and the camera will record a remarkably steady picture throughout.

Any professional crew will have one person – the production assistant – whose job it is to log all the shots, with details of their timings, the faults – if any – and any other comments. But another vital piece of information to help find a particular shot quickly when editing is the time-code reading on the recorder.

Essentially, a time code is a set of figures which can be used to record the number of the tape being used, and the time in minutes seconds and frames from the start of the tape. This information is generated in the recorder and it's recorded on the tape in an area which isn't used for picture or audio information. Later, when the tape is replayed on the edit suite, that time code can be read and displayed as the tape runs – so a note of the coding for a particular shot can be entered into the edit machine, the correct cassette can be inserted, and the machine will find the shot automatically.

This makes it possible to edit in two stages. The initial edit can be done very simply on a two-machine edit suite, even on the VHS format. Usually this means copying the camera original tapes, which will have been recorded on U-Matic, 1-inch, Hi-Band MII or Betacam or any of the other broadcast or semi-broadcast formats, on to VHS cassettes with the time-code actually showing as a set of figures on the bottom of the picture. This means shots can be identified on the original tapes, and on the programme tape built up during editing, as a series of time-code readings.

Once the time-consuming business of building up the pro-gramme tape, which involves all the creative decisions, has been finished, that first edited tape, called the offline edit, can be used to control the machines which build up the actual master tape on one of the more expensive broadcast quality formats. This time, of course, the time codes won't appear in the picture, but the ma-chines will be reading the information and acting on it, to copy the offline tape in what is called the online edit. At this stage, the special effects are added and the sound-track mixed. The copying of the original edit can be done entirely by computer. Today's online suites can take each cassette and make all the edits from that cassette in the right places on the programme tape, entirely by themselves. Then the cassette is replaced by another of the original tapes, and so on, and so on. This means a complex programme which may have taken weeks to edit at the offline stage can be online edited in as many days – which saves money as the equip-ment is costly to run.

PROMOTION

The corporate video is one of the most lucrative areas of television production. At its highest level, it might attract broadcast levels of budget and broadcast standards of picture quality. At the bottom end of the corporate ladder, many a local company might want to draw attention to itself and its capabilities through a promotional video. However, if you intend to enter this market, you'll have to take the first step towards true professionalism. This means budgeting a production, pricing your services and the use of your equipment at a realistic rate.

In most cases, your customers will know what they want their programmes to say. But remember that you are the video professional, and it's part of your job to advise them on how their message can best be put. Take the length of the programme. This will depend on the interest it will carry for the chosen audience but as a general rule-of-thumb a corporate video should be about twenty minutes. If all the shooting is straightforward, in local premises, then you could shoot a ten-minute programme in two days. But if one of those days involves shooting out of doors, then how critical would bad weather be? Do they want a presenter, or voice-over from start to finish? An on-screen presenter may lend an extra gloss, but he or she will be more expensive than a voice-over. Check their rates and include them in the budget as a separate item, with one or two cheaper alternatives. Cost your own research. Visit each location to make a list of worthwhile shots. Check that you have someone with you when you're shooting, to make sure that the picture you record is what they want their customers to see including the finer details. Most companies will want a word from the boss. If he's not a natural performer, ask him to read his piece as a voice-over. But few things are as convincing as a genuinely happy customer – either vox-pops from people leaving a store to statements from major clients.

Go for the surprising and entertaining ingredients in whatever the company wants to say about itself. Concentrate on the positive qualities. Keep it light – and remember that understated pride is often better than shouting the company message at your audience at full volume.

INDEX

CLOSE UP SOLUTIONS

The top picture on page 41 is one of those awkward shots, made up of several different elements – too close for a long shot, but not concentrating on one particular subject in close-up. Better to close-in on either the sign (1) as a potential cutaway, or the clock (2) as an indication through your programme of the passing of time, or the official notice on the wall (3) for its period flavour, or the waiting passenger (4) – provided he looks away from the camera.

The middle picture is an example of the classic long-shot – but nothing is moving. A closer framing on the background would allow you to avoid the repair work in the left foreground by angling the camera more to the right (1). On the other hand, if the work in progress was part of the story you were telling, then you would need to make it the centre of your picture (2). The lack of movement is a different problem – you could avoid it by concentrating on the rhythm of the overhead signs (3), or you could make a feature of it by zooming right in to the clock and the station entrance (4). This allows you to make two points with a single shot – it's midday, and it's quiet. Alternatively, if you wait long enough, you may find people entering or leaving the station through the doorway give you the movement you're looking for.

Time here for some quick reactions, based on what you've shot, or what you think your next shot is going to be, after this one. If you've just been watching the band of the Rifle regiment (the dark uniforms marching into frame from right to left), then you could frame your picture around them and pan to follow them off the parade square (1). Another possibility is to frame the shot as tightly as you can on the point where the two bands will march through one another (2), and keep the camera still, so the screen is filled with groups of moving faces, passing one another in opposite directions. But if your next shot is likely to be the Fusiliers band (in the red coats), the corporal with the Regimental mascot (3) is a natural focal point. Frame the shot tightly around him, pan to follow him on to the parade ground, and then zoom out to reveal the rest of the band, once they're clear of the background and the light is in the right direction for a good wide shot.